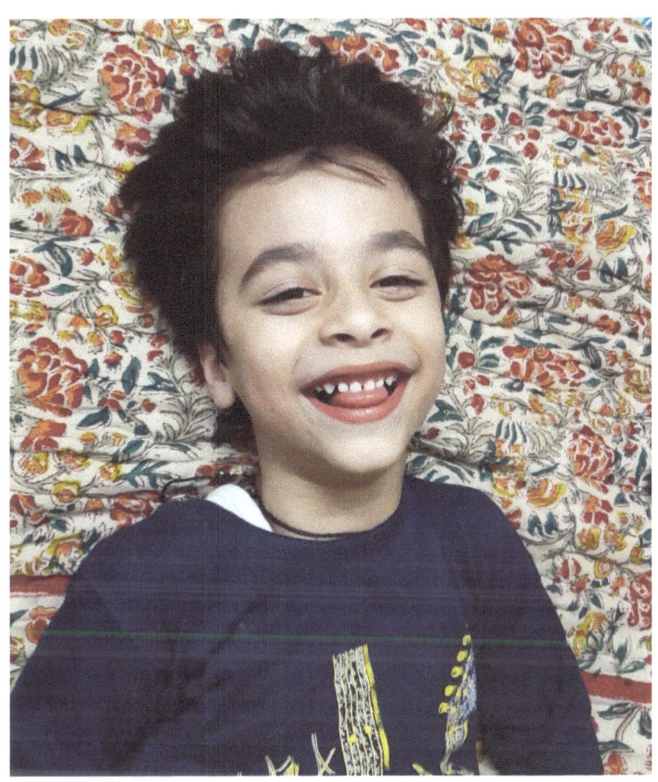

Dedicated to Vihaan

Brahm se Brahmaand

Journey from Outerself to Innerself

Forwarded by Kunwar Shekhar Vijendra
Co-founder & Chancellor of Shobhit University

The Complete Science Behind Sound Healing

DR. ANJU SHARMA

INDIA • SINGAPORE • MALAYSIA

ISBN 979-8-88704-900-7

ADVANCE PRAISE FOR THE BOOK

Sound will be the medicine for the future; we cannot stop the vibration to spread. Sound is not a new topic. It is an ancient topic—*nadayoga* which is sound healing should be researched for it will travel everywhere. The Sound of Infinity Band and Dr Anju Sharma together have done a beautiful demonstration at the Second and Third National Wellbeing Summit organized by Shobhit University. We are enlightened by the vibrations of the sound performed during the sound session and hopefully, we will do research in the field of *nadayoga* too.

KUNWAR SHEKHAR VIJENDER
HON'BLE CHANCELLOR, SHOBHIT UNIVERSITY, MEERUT (U.P.)

Very relaxing and soothing sound session. It helped in reducing the work pressure and mental stress; we are looking forward to having more sessions of sound healing.

MAX TOWER, NOIDA (U.P.)

During the time of the COVID-19 lockdown, Dr Anju Sharma created a lot of awareness through social media platforms, regarding mental health through sound healing sessions. She also helped a lot of people to come out of their various issues related to mental health. For her dedication, 94.3 My FM, Jaipur, honoured her work.

94.3 MY FM JAIPUR, RAJASTHAN

For the first time in the history of the courtroom, a sound healing session was performed, where all the vibrations coming from the sound instrument vibrated in the courtroom. The session was performed for district judges and judges, easing their mental pressure and they were given some techniques to handle their stress. This meditation session was to ease the mental pressure and create awareness for understanding the body language through sound healing. In the presence of the district and session judge along with other senior judges, Dr Anju Sharma and her team created a different heavenly aura in the courtroom.

DISTRICT LEGAL SERVICES AUTHORITY
NORTH-NORTHWEST ROHINI COURT,
ROHINI, NEW DELHI

Sound healing session and motivational talk to the prisoners along with some intensive therapies has been done by Dr Anju Sharma on how to reduce the stress level of the convicts and help them to understand more clearly their life. It was a fruitful session for all the people present in the jail.

SUPERINTENDENT OF TIHAR JAIL NO. 8
TIHAR JAIL, NEW DELHI

TABLE OF CONTENTS

FOREWORD

The ancient *Mandukya Upanishad* describes AUM in considerable detail as the sound-body of the Universe: "AUM is this imperishable Word, AUM is the Universe, and this is the exposition of AUM. The past, the present and the future, all that was, all that is, all that will be, is AUM. Likewise all else that may exist beyond the bounds of Time, that too is AUM. All this Universe is the Eternal Brahman, this Self is the Eternal, and the Self is fourfold." *(Sri Aurobindo, The Upanishads, Mandukya Upanishad 1-2, pg. 319)*

Modern day scientists, attempting to capture the sounds of the universe and the planet have recorded the vibratory patterns of the planet as well as the 'big bang" of the creation of the universe, and converted them into sounds. Science is still catching up to understanding how sound heals, but the current research is promising. A review of 400 published scientific articles on music as medicine found strong evidence that music has mental and physical health benefits in improving mood and reducing stress. In fact, it is well proven that certain sounds can bring about a calming and focusing influence that is palpable.

More or less this understanding is taken up as the science of sound-healing by various self-help masters and practitioners at different platforms for obtaining for their audience peace of mind, stress-free life, and balancing of emotions.

Dr. Anju Sharma in this book brings out and establishes the need and the ways of obtaining such a cleansing process through concentrating on sound and while enjoying this experience. Standing somewhere between the ancient wisdom of the sound systems of the eternity, creation and its subtle connections with the working of our body and levels of environment; and, the present-day talk of the universe in a non-spiritual way, Dr. Sharma recommends that healing of the body- even physical, and mental disturbances is possible by the opening up of the body and mind to different sounds.

Taking cues from various experimentations trending in the world, she attempts to make this sound-based exalted sense of our connection and transaction with our larger environment, an every-day business of the yoga of healing. This self-help book will help those who are in search of methods to heal themselves through the yoga of practice with sound.

I wish the writer and reader a happy journey in the sound-space of their sensual and spiritual life.

Kunwar Shekhar Vijendra

Co-founder & Chancellor of Shobhit University -Publisher)

PREFACE

Everything in this universe is in vibration—you tune your body like you tune your instrument. When an instrument is not in tune, the sound that comes through that instrument will be unbearable as opposed to a tuned instrument which gives out a soothing sound. Different instruments are set to certain frequencies—some vibrations give productive impact and some are unproductive. Those vibrations that give an unproductive impact can cause problems in our bodies.

Sound healing allows your body to heal itself by slowing down your brain waves which affect every cell in your body shifting them from **disease** to **ease.**

The journey of the sound vibration into sound healing is sound therapy, which helps the individual to get a fair idea about their disease and helps them to recover better.

Sound therapy is the journey of vibrations which not only creates awareness but also bring enlightenment, from *naadbrahma* to *brahmanand.*

ACKNOWLEDGEMENT

I would like to acknowledge my research work on sound healing therapy and dedicate this to my parents, my brother, my mentors, and my gurus under whose guidance and support this divine learning of sound healing came into my life.

I would like to dedicate this book to the strength behind all my work: Vihaan.

I would like to thank Dr Biindu Khuraana, Shri Kunwar Shekhar Vijendra, and Mr Chhatrapal Singh Shekhawat who encouraged and motivated me to create awareness regarding sound healing and write it in the form of research work so that this divine knowledge could spread among everyone.

Last but not least, I would like to thank all my patients, friends, and well-wishers who trusted me and gave me so much love and motivation to complete this work.

I would also like to acknowledge the Universe and the Almighty for supporting me to complete my research work on time.

01

INTRODUCTION TO SOUND HEALING

1.1 Sound Healing

Sound healing which is known as sound therapy has been practised since ancient times. The concept of sound therapy is based on the idea that everybody creates a vibration that is resonant in a certain way. We can also say vibrational healing is based on the idea that everything in the universe including our body is in the state of vibration.

Out-of-balance body results in illness. This illness is caused by blockage, which stops the organ in question from vibrating at its healthy/optimum frequency.

Sound healing works by sending sound waves throughout your body, which brings harmony through oscillation and resonance. This helps restore your body balance, which in turn helps you heal, known as the magical healing of sound therapy. Sound healing is majorly considered a new-age wellness therapy but it is not a new form of therapy. This therapy goes back to ancient Greek times when music was used to cure psychological conditions.

Sound therapy was used to stimulate and boost morale. It was believed that sound can heal the body because humans have an instinct for sounds and that is why people still prefer to listen to music to feel better and lift their mood.

Everything in the universe has a vibrational frequency including the human body. And frequencies of sound impact both the body and mind. No wonder why certain songs often create a specific type of emotion within us.

Sound healing is an age-old healing procedure that uses frequencies to bring the body into vibrational balance and harmony during therapy.

In a sound therapy session, typically a person lies down on the floor and listens to a variety of instruments played by a sound practitioner; the lying down person experiences vibrations of many sounds as he/she is bathing in soothing vibrations. The frequencies of these sounds slow down brainwaves to a healing stage. Some of the various instruments that are used during sound therapy are singing bowls, tuning forks, Tibetan bowls, gongs, and drums. The crystal bowls are tuned to heal the seven chakras. The gong helps to release the tension from the body and stimulates the system.

1.2 Types of Sounds

There are different types of sounds including audible sound, inaudible sound, pleasant sound, soft and loud noise, and rhythmic music.

The sound produced by the piano is soft, audible, and musical, similarly, the traffic sound is a loud sound that is unpleasant to our ears.

There are three categories of sound:

Infrasonic sound is a sound with a frequency of less than 20 Hz. Elephant uses infrasonic sounds to interact with other elephants hundreds of kilometres away. Infrasonic are the sounds that are below the rhythm of human frequency and they come under inaudible sounds.

Sonic sound is a sound with a frequency between 20 Hz and 20000 Hz; all the sounds which we hear fall under this and are further categorized into **verbal sonic** and **nonverbal sonic.**

Verbal sonic sound is that which is produced by the collision of two objects together like the sound of an air conditioning fan, an aeroplane taking off, a balloon popping, a buzzing bee, etc.

Non-verbal sonic sounds are those which come into our bodies through our thoughts and assumptions. These sounds disturb a person the most, it can turn into a form of anxiety, bipolarity, and many more psychosomatic disorders.

Ultrasonic sound is the third category of sound with a frequency of more than 20000Hz. We need special equipment to hear sounds like ultrasonic devices. Radiologists use ultrasonic machines or devices to listen to these sounds—like to hear the heartbeat and assess the growth of a foetus in the mother's womb.

1.3 Characteristics of Sound

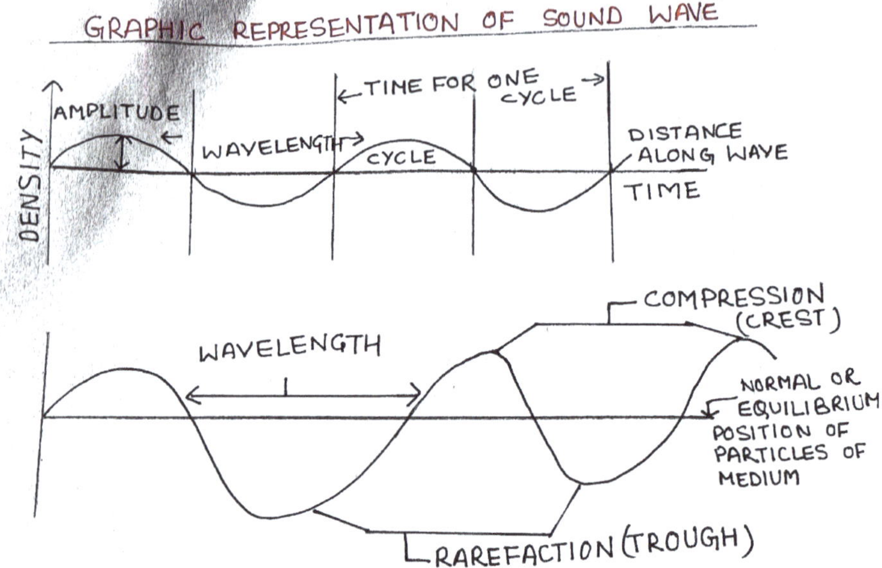

A sound is a form of energy just like electricity, heat, or light. When you strike a bell it makes a loud ringing noise. Now try putting a finger on the bell after you have struck it… you can feel it shaking; this to-and-fro motion is termed vibration.

The sound moves through a medium by alternatively contracting and expanding, which creates a minute pressure difference that we perceive as sound. Let's discuss the characteristics of sound waves like amplitude, frequency, wavelength, etc. We hear all sorts of noises—shouting, laughing, crying, talking all of which are not just restricted to humans; animals also make noise and these are distinctly different from the human voice.

We know a drum does not make the same sound like a flute. So how does the difference come about? Let's explore some of the basic properties of the sound wave to understand this.

When sound waves are represented in a waveform, we instantly notice some basic characteristics. The waveform is a pictorial representation of the pressure variation in the air which travels as sound. These waves are alternative regions of high pressure and low pressure. Thanks to the waveform, sound wave now seems very similar to light, which is another electromagnetic radiation.

Amplitude

Amplitude in light refers to the amount of energy in an electromagnetic wave. It also refers to the distance of the maximum vertical displacement of the wave from its mean position.

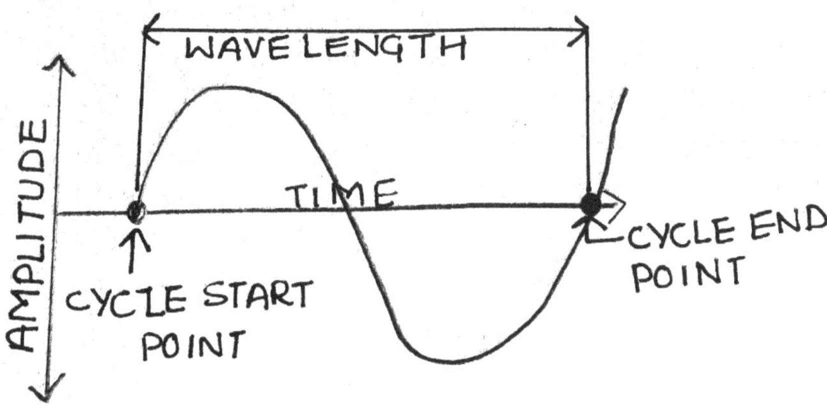

The larger the amplitude, the higher the energy, which refers to the magnitude of the compression and expansion of the medium. This amplitude of the sound wave is perceived by our ears as loudness.

Frequency or pitch of the sound waves

The frequency, also known as the pitch, of a sound wave refers to the rate of vibration of the sound travelling through the air. The parameters decide whether a sound is perceived as a higher pitch in sound.

The frequency of the vibration is calculated in cycles per second. The standard unit for the frequency is Hz, its definition being 1/T, where "T" refers to the time period of the wave (it is the time required for the wave to complete one cycle).

The wavelength and frequency of a sound wave can be mathematically represented as

The velocity of the sound = frequency X wavelength

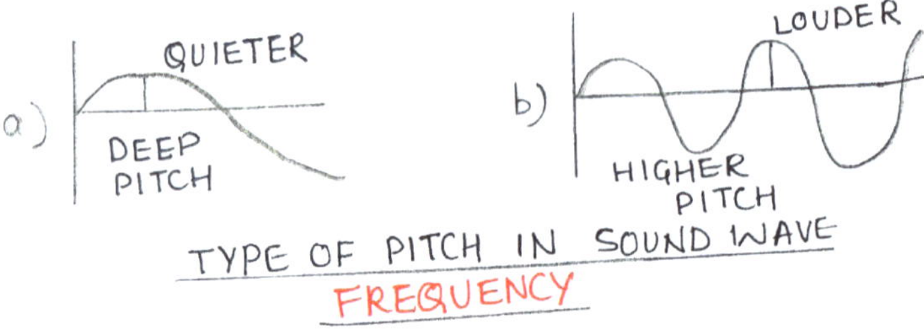

The below graph can be used for understanding more about sound.

The first graph represents a sound wave from a drum while the second graph represents the sound wave from a whistle; you already know the difference in the sound but notice the difference in their frequencies.

Wavelength

The waveform representation converts the pressure vibration of the sound wave into a pictorial graph, which is easier to understand. A sound wave is made of an area of high pressure alternated by an area of low pressure.

The high-pressure area is represented as the peak of the graph, the low-pressure area is represented as the top of the graph. The physical distance between two consecutive peaks in a sound wave is referred to as the wavelength of the sound wave.

1.4 Advantages and Disadvantages of Sound Healing

Advantages of sound as therapy:

1. **Relaxes our mind**: One of the greatest benefits and advantages of sound therapy is that it relieves stress and relaxes the mind and it retunes the brain to cope with any kind of stress.

2. **Clears energy blockages**: The deep feeling during the sound therapy session opens and clears the chakras and releases stuck energies. Sound therapy sends stimulating vibration to the brain that encourages the brain to release suppressed energy. During this healing, you feel a physical sense like a twinkling effect or feel different body temperature like hot or cold; at this time focus on your breathing and allow the sense to pass.
3. **Boost your immunity system**: Sound therapy helps in healing physically, mentally, emotionally, and spiritually. The holistic healing improves our immunity and helps the body to fight against any diseases. It also clears the mind and leads to a new feeling of happiness and well-being.
4. **Improves attention span**: Many parents consider sound therapy for their kids to improve their attention span. Also, those facing speech difficulties have found a great solution in sound therapy as some frequencies enable the brain to listen more effectively and focus the mind on a certain task.
5. **Helps in improving relationships**: Too much stress and tension can impact relationships, be it personal or professional. With sound healing, the stress level is controlled and the mind relaxes to help build better relationships with others.
6. **Pain relief**: Many people use sound therapy to get relief from chronic headaches, migraines, and body pain. It can also address the underlying cause of many pains like stress or high BP. One study reported that adults who suffered from migraine got relief from their symptoms after two weeks of sound therapy. It works like magic on pain as it targets the root cause of the problem.
7. **Boosts confidence and focus**: It creates new positive patterns in your brain. Sound therapy can also give you a great confidence boost as it helps you to regain focus in your life. This is achieved by lowering brain wave frequency to help you to focus more.
8. **Increases energy**: Much of the way you feel is connected to the signals that your brain sends throughout the body. Sound therapy

feeds the brain with stimulating sounds that motivate the brain to release latent energy.

9. **Help think clearly and improves organization skill**: By using specific frequencies to help rebalance brain functions sound therapy can help you think clearly and avoid the temptation to depend on self-destructive and addictive habits. It also improves your organizational skills, which will benefit your work and family life too.
10. **Promotes a healthy mind**: It promotes a healthy body and you can break the cycle of negative thinking and habits to enjoy a much calmer and focused life.

The disadvantage of sound healing:

In some cases, sound therapy can lead to sleep disturbance, or trigger unwanted memories. It can cause increased anxiety for some and is not advised for dementia patients and in general old people. People having high blood pressure are also not advised to undergo sound therapy as it may increase the flow of energy, which can, in turn, increase the blood pressure or even lead to cardiovascular issues. Sometimes it's seen that noise explosion can also affect the heart rate of the foetus in the mother's womb.

Everything in this universe has its advantage and disadvantage. Sound is an easy solution to our problems and clearly, its advantages outweigh its disadvantages.

1.5 How is Sound Healing Effective in Day-to-Day Life?

When your body is out of balance disease can result. Illness is caused by blockages, which stop the organ in question from vibrating at its healthy frequencies. Sound healing works by sending sound waves throughout your body, which brings harmony through oscillation and resonance of the cell—this helps restore your body's balance which in turn helps you heal.

These days many practitioners believe that the use of these bowls can have a significant beneficial effect on the healing of your mind and body, especially when combined with positive affirmation in the form of mantras and chants.

This therapy is believed to directly affect your brain wave activity supporting and improving your state of consciousness.

02

PURPOSE OF SOUND HEALING

2.1 The Purpose

One of the most common health problems is noise-induced hearing loss (NIHL). Exposure to loud noise can also cause high blood pressure, heart diseases, sleep disturbance, and stress which turns into psychological as well as physiological problems. This problem can affect all age groups, especially children, women, and old people.

One psychological study examines evidence of the health benefit of natural soundscape and quantifies the prevalence of the restorative acoustic environments in natural parks across the United States. The result affirms that natural sounds improve health, increase the positive effect, and lower stress and annoyance.

Sound affects our bodies both psychologically and physiologically in powerful ways because hearing is our primary warning sense. Any sudden sound starts a process that

- releases cortisol
- increase the heart rate
- changes the breathing pattern

Sound can produce some of the strongest emotional reactions in humans as well as in animals, whether it's happiness, sadness, fear, or nostalgia.

Sound is a series of vibrations that travel into the ear and gets converted into electrical signals that are sent to the brain by the vestibulocochlear nerve.

According to researchers, listening to any kind of sound such as music or noise has a significant effect on our moods and emotions because of brain dopamine regulation—a neurotransmitter strongly involved in emotional behaviour and mood regulation.

Sound allows the body to heal itself by slowing down brain waves which affect every cell in the body shifting them from dis-ease to being at ease.

2.2 Benefits of Sound Healing

Sound healing helps you clear energetic blockages and facilitates healing on a physical and mental level. During the COVID 19 pandemic, sound and music therapy miraculously helped in lowering stress for many people.

Here are some of the benefits of sound therapy:

- Fewer mood swings
- Lower body pressure
- Lower stress
- Brings calmness
- Lower cholesterol level
- Better pain management
- Reduces risk of stroke and coronary arteries diseases
- Improved sleep
- Increases focus and concentration
- Helps in meditation
- Decrease in anxiety level
- Helps in dealing with loneliness
- Lifts depression
- Helps in improving breathing
- Create awareness of the body

The harmonizing effect produced by the sound creates a soothing effect throughout the entire body. When different sound vibrations and frequencies are created, it impacts the body and its meridians helping promote deep relaxation, release emotional trauma, and relieve stress and anxiety.

2.3 How Cells Grow Back Through Sound

Generally speaking, low-frequency waves are linked to "delta" and "theta" states, which can boost relaxation and improve sleep.

Higher frequencies reportedly boost the brain waves into a "gamma state", which may make you more alert or better able to recall memory; it can reduce the tension of cells and promote relaxation.

It is more effective than prescription drugs in reducing stress levels before surgery.

A study published in 2017 found that 30 minutes of sound therapy combined with traditional care after spinal surgery reduces stress and helps our cells repair and sometimes regrow.

Can sound waves damage brain cells?

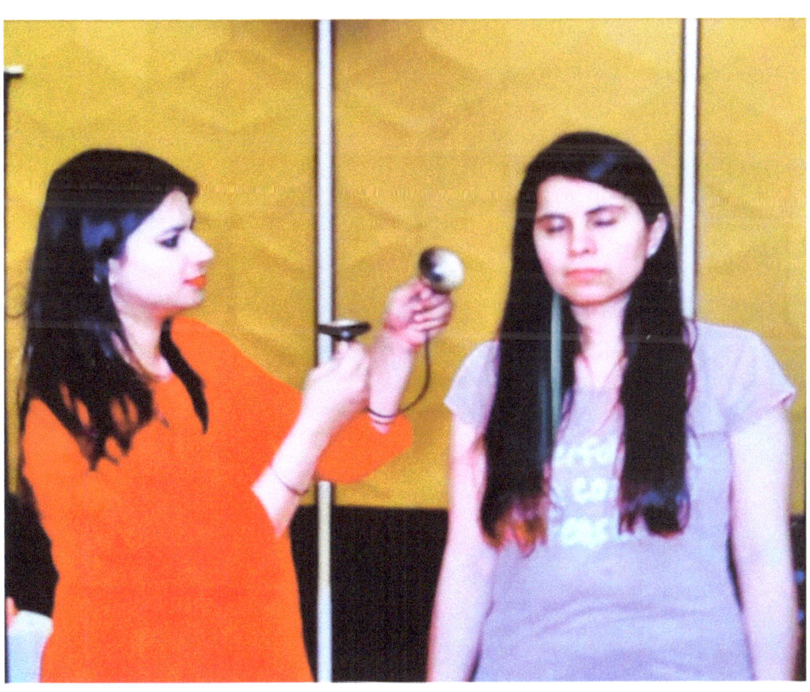

Prolonged exposure to loud noise alters how the brain processes speech, potentially increasing the difficulty in distinguishing speech sounds. According to neuroscientists, exposure to intensely loud sounds can lead to permanent damage to the hair cells, which act as sound receivers in the ear.

2.4 How Sound Energy Helps in Healing Physical, Mental, Emotional, and Spiritual Wellbeing

Any thought which enters the body is in the form of vibrations which contains an electric charge, which creates disturbance inside the body in the form of illness. The vibration travels inside the body through the opening channel of the body like ears, eyes, nose, skin, mouth, and especially through the ears and skin because skin and ears can hear the sound frequency of 20 Hz to 20000 Hz.

Most of these verbal sounds and non-verbal sounds can create a movement in the cell through an electric charge. So we can say that when there is any movement in the cell, it causes disturbance in the emotion as emotion is energy + motion (movement). Any energy which is in a movement creates either a productive reaction or disturbance in the body; so if the energy is not moving, then there is no vibration too.

It can cause stagnant energy which can also create problems. So any flowing energy inside the body which is coming from the outer source through the opening channel can cause a problem at the physical or the emotional level. When the emotions are not taken care of, it reaches the physical level. So the first step of any problem in the body is through the emotion (the vibrational mode)—it reaches the emotion then it reaches the mental level.

When the emotions are not cleared it can create a problem on the mental level which we see in the form of psychological disorders like depression, manic, bipolarity, anxiety, and hypertension and later affects physical health too.

So, sound healing as therapy helps to create first awareness regarding the vibration entering the body, which helps us to understand the various signs of the body. So when any kind of vibrational thought enters the body first, it travels through the auditory nerves of the ear and then to the brain, from where through the electromagnetic charge the message and the information are transmitted to the entire body.

Electric current passing through our body responds according to the vibrations which are coming from the external source and that's how behaviour and personality are formed.

Once the problem or an illness is identified, sound healing not only helps us to develop the connection between the emotional, mental, and physical well-being but also helps us to develop the connection between the external and internal world and by which we can develop our spiritual channel as it helps us to create the awareness of the body.

The universal sound therapy first heals at the emotional level, then the mental level, and when the energy movement heals the mental blockage, it automatically helps us in clearing the physical health. Once all the three levels are taken care of, it then connects us with the sound of the universe which we called the *nada*—the passage of *nadayoga* through *Brahma Nada* is the journey of emotional well-being to spiritual well-being or in other words from dis-ease to being at ease.

03

HISTORY OF SOUND ENERGY

3.1 Who Discovered Sound Energy?

Leonardo Da Vinci, the famous Italian thinker and artist is usually credited with the discovery that sound moves in waves. In 1490, Leonardo Da Vinci inserted a tube into the water to study underwater acoustics and tested for signals from a ship with his ears.

However, it was Galileo Galilei (1564-1642), to whom the study of vibrations and the correlation between pitch and frequency of the sound wave is attributed to. This was a very significant discovery.

Later on, Alexander Graham Bell transmitted the first sound vibration between two receivers in 1875. In the 17th century, the French scientist and philosopher Pierre Gassendi made the earliest known measurement of the speed of the sound in the air.

3.2 The Origin of Sound

Sound waves are generated by sound sources such as the vibrating diaphragm of a stereo speaker. The sound source creates vibration in the surrounding medium. As the source continues to vibrate the medium the vibration propagates away from the source at the speed of sound thus forming the sound waves.

Sound is a type of energy made by vibration. When an object vibrates, it causes movement in the surrounding air molecule; these molecules bump into the molecules closer to them causing them to vibrate and this gives rise to the sound vibrations.

3.3 The First Sound in the Universe

BIG BANG THEORY (the first sound of the universe)

Around 13.7 billion years ago, everything in the entire universe was condensed in an infinitely small singularity, a point of infinite denseness and heat. Suddenly an explosive expansion began, ballooning our universe faster than the speed of light. The explosion produced a lot of light and sound simultaneously with high speed.

The Big Bang that gave birth to our universe was not some explosive sound. Instead, it was more akin to a robotic humming—a continuous rhythmic hum with an equal and proper interval of time.

Science tells us that the universe began with a big bang, whereas the Vedas say that the Big Bang is actually OM, which is not a one-time phenomenon but rather a continuous sound. In fact, if the OM stopped for even a microsecond, the whole universe as we know would disappear instantly.

OM rises from pure consciousness.

3.4 Sound Vibrations as Nadayoga

The Vedic reference to *nadayoga*, OM, is mentioned numerous times throughout Vedic literature most commonly in its original form of AUM.

The knowledge of the four Vedas (Rig, Yajur, Sama, and Atharva) is contained in the Rig Veda and all the information of the Rig Veda is contained in the first syllable, which is the beginning of the mantra AUM.

According to the ancient puranic texts, AUM represents the union of three main masculine deities and the forces within the universe.

"A" means Brahma the creation
"U" means Vishnu the maintenance
"M" means Shiva the destruction.

In the Bhagavad Gita, Lord Krishna says, "Of words I am OM".

The Chandogya Upanishad opens with the recommendation to "let's meditate on OM, the essence of all". The Chandogya Upanishad also tells us that the Gods took the song OM unto themselves thinking with this song "We shall overcome the demons" implying that OM inspires the good inclination within each person.

The Katha Upanishad says when we chant OM with sincerity, the Brahman (the Absolute Universe) listens to us. Whatever the individual desires, he gets that.

The Shvestashvatra Upanishad says that OM is the power given to us to know more about the Supreme Power or the divinity or the Atma within oneself.

Adi Shankara said that if only one Upanishad had to be studied, then it should be the Mandukya Upanishad because it entirely is devoted to understanding OM. It also supports that OM or AUM is the whole world—all your past, present, and future, whatever exists, beyond and before time. The Mandukya Upanishad also talks about four states of consciousness, the sound of the universe, and the sound of self.

- The first stage is represented by the letter **"A"** by knowing that we all become masters of our senses fulfilling all our desires. This stage is "the walking stage" where we know how to manifest and also know more about the desire where the sensors are turned outward.
- The second stage is the stage where we go deep represented by the letter **"U"**. In this stage, we command our body to travel inside. This stage is also known as the "dream stage" where we direct all our thoughts inwards.
- The third stage is the bridge and the consciousness between the external and internal matter. The third stage of "deep sleep" where consciousness enjoys peace with no perception of anything is represented by the letter the **"M"**. The Mandukya Upanishad says

beautifully about this stage that everything merges into ourselves through us.

- In Patanjali Yoga Sutra, it is mentioned that **M**, "Mmmmm" is the sound of self, and is the name of God (finding the God in self). It also mentions that "God gives truth to his beloved in sleep".
- The Mandukya Upanishad states the fourth stage is "*turiya*", which means
- transcendental consciousness, or the Atma, the soundless aspect of **AUM** or gap between thoughts. Turiya is represented by AUM; it is the combination of three sounds though it is invisible. AUM is the sound that deals with the Self, beyond birth and death; it is the symbol and the sound of everlasting joy. This sound is about knowing and entering "the self within the self"—those who know the Truth become the Truth. This sound of the universe is both external and internal and within this is the ongoing process of creation, destruction and manifestation.

Practising the Nadayoga

As OM is the sound of the universe it's always present in the universe. It is the sound which is going on continuously in the universe. So technically, we can't produce this sound. We can't create OM by chanting it, we can only produce vibrations, which are synergic to the vibration that already exists in the universe, which is OM. It is not a mere chant made by us or initiated by us, instead of that we can maintain a connection between our Self and the Supreme Reality or we can say the connection between the universe and self, which is manifested can be created by the sound vibration in the form of OM.

An alternative way of chanting OM connects the *Nadayoga* to *Brahma Nada* in one breath: **Aaaaaaaaaa-Uuuuuuuu-Mmmmmmm** followed by silence.

The fullness of **"A"** sound collapses into **"U"** and then into **"M"** and, finally, the silence of all three together immerses into Brahman; the whole is inside you. All the four stages of life, that is, the waking stage, the dreaming stage, and the deep sleep stage finally merge into the fourth stage or the absolute oneness or the *turiya*.

This is a journey from the external to the internal universe— from the *Nada to Brahmanada*.

(Sometimes if you sit very quietly, you can even hear the sound of OM like a distant cosmic hmmmmm… listen within yourself. It's not outside you, it is within you.

3.5 Does Our Planet Produce or Make Sound?

Sound travels in waves like light or heat do, but unlike them, sound travels by making molecules vibrate on earth. Sound travel to your ears by vibrating air molecules. In space, there are no molecules to vibrate in the larger space between stars and planets, hence there is no sound.

Planets do emit radiations, which can produce sounds that can be heard. The sound of the universe is carried by vibrations in space-time called gravitational waves.

When astronauts are out in space, they can whistle, talk or even yell inside their space suit, but the other astronaut would not hear the noise because there is nothing out in the space (like an atmosphere). The sound waves from one astronaut's whistle cannot travel over to another astronaut's ear because there is no molecule particle present in the space. Hence we can say for sound to be heard, the atmosphere should be present.

04

TYPE OF SOUND HEALING THERAPY

There are many types of sound healing therapies which we normally perform in our workshops. Some therapies are performed in group sessions and some therapies are performed one-on-one depending on the disease.

Both the group and personal therapies work miraculously on the patient. When performed in a repeated pattern, whether a person wants it or not, the sound vibrations travel inside the body and help the person get better. Some of the major therapies are mentioned below.

4.1 Sound Healing Trauma Therapy

This therapy is specially designed in a manner where the person can release their trauma. So before understanding the therapy we should understand trauma.

According to the American Psychological Association (APA), trauma is an emotional response to a terrible event like an accident or natural disaster. However, a person may experience trauma as a response to any event defined as physically or emotionally threatening or harmful.

Sound healing therapy is mostly used for relaxing the mind, body, and soul. In this therapy specifically, the body cells remove the pain and suffering because it is believed that once the deep-rooted problem resolves the pain of the trauma, suffering will also get resolved. The intensity of the trauma makes it alive all the time, especially whenever the memory of the pain or suffering is triggered again.

In this process, we work with the Himalayan and Tibetan sound healing to release the pain and suffering of a particular cell where the trauma is set. Sometimes, the healing is more difficult than the trauma because the person has to go through all the pain again. Through the sound bowl, we give vibrational intensity, which allows or gives pressure on the cells, pain or suffering to go away and allow the body to release or let go of all the pain from the body.

Every trauma has its path from beginning to end. Sound healing therapy turns the trauma into an incident and then helps the person to let it go. In the final stage, the higher vibrations and frequency clean and repair the cells, making them regrow them to build the opportunity to grow a beautiful life and remove the imprints of the trauma slowly and slowly.

Method: In the trauma healing workshop, sound healing bowls are used according to the type and intensity of the trauma.

According to research, every trauma consists of four major issues:

- survival
- guilt
- acceptance
- having no clarity

And according to each issue, different sound healing bowls with different frequency is used.

Root chakra bowl: “F” node

Solar plexus bowl: “G” node

Throat chakra bowl: “A” node

Third eye chakra bowl: “E” node

These are the four bowls that are mostly used for all the trauma from big to small. These are the basic four major issues or problems that give rise to other problems and emotional blockages. So first in any trauma healing, we use these four chakra balls and then according to the releasing process of the therapy we change the ball and their intensity. We always start with the 100% intensity on the bowl with the help of a mallet and end with one per cent intensity leading to calming vibrations.

This therapy normally takes 35 to 45 minutes according to the intensity of the trauma although one can see visible changes in a body in the first two sessions itself. In the workshop, we also train the participants to perform trauma healing therapies as the advanced form of sound healing therapy where we constantly observe every single movement of the body.

This therapy gives complete relaxation and clears the deep-rooted problems inside the body. It benefits both psychologically and physiologically.

Process and Preparation

In trauma sound healing therapy, the patient has to lie down on the floor in a comfortable position. Make sure the patient's back is on the floor and his breathing is normal. The patient is then asked to focus on his breathing and at the same time, four bowls are placed around his body. These are the root chakra 'F' node bowl, solar plexus chakra 'G' node bowl, throat chakra 'A' note bowl, and the third eye chakra 'E' note bowl. With the help of mallets strike the bowl with the intensity from 100% to 10%.

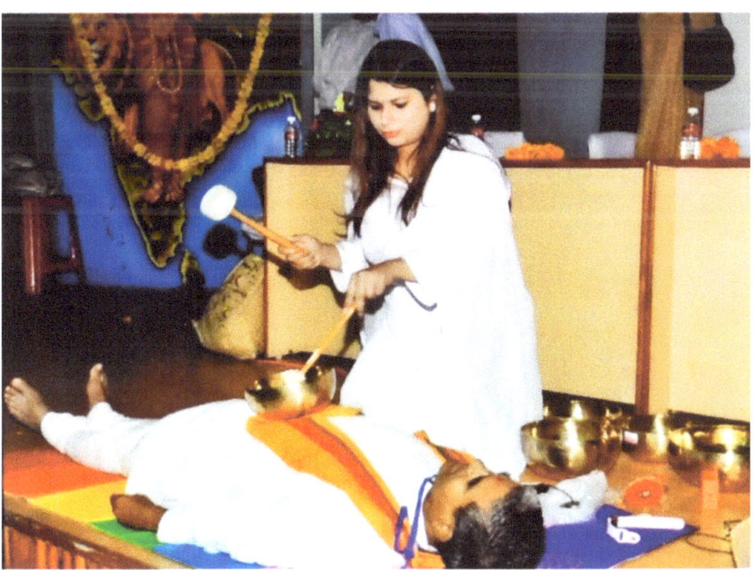

Repeat the process continuously for 35 to 45 minutes; according to the reaction and observation during the therapy, keep changing the bowls and continue the process. Trauma healing therapy helps and allows the cells which are rigid to become loose as the vibrations coming from the sound bowls help repair the cells which are broken and distorted.

4.2 Pain-Management Sound Healing Therapy

This therapy is the most important in sound healing. In this therapy, we pick the exact area of the problem and then accordingly we put the bowl related to the chakras and start the therapy. In pain management therapy, we directly put the sound healing bowl connected to the targeted area.

So here, first, we have to understand the pain, which is nothing but the inflammation of the cells caused due to trauma. The pain reduction sound therapy works magically in reducing the intensity of the pain and repairing the blockages of the cells through the vibrations produced by the sound healing bowl.

Pain management therapy is further divided into two parts:

- **Cold press sound therapy**: In this, a bowl is kept on the targeted area where there is inflammation or pain. We put pressure on the area through the bowl and rotate it clockwise and anticlockwise. This technique massages the cells so that pain and inflammation subside and the cells get back to their original form.
- **Hot water press therapy**: In this, hot water is used for healing. This is done in two ways:

    a. In the first method, hot water is put in the bowl and the targeted area is massaged with it. The process is repeated for 10 to 15 minutes.

    b. In the second method, a mallet is struck on the hot water bowl with different intensities. Care must be taken not to spill the hot water on the body.

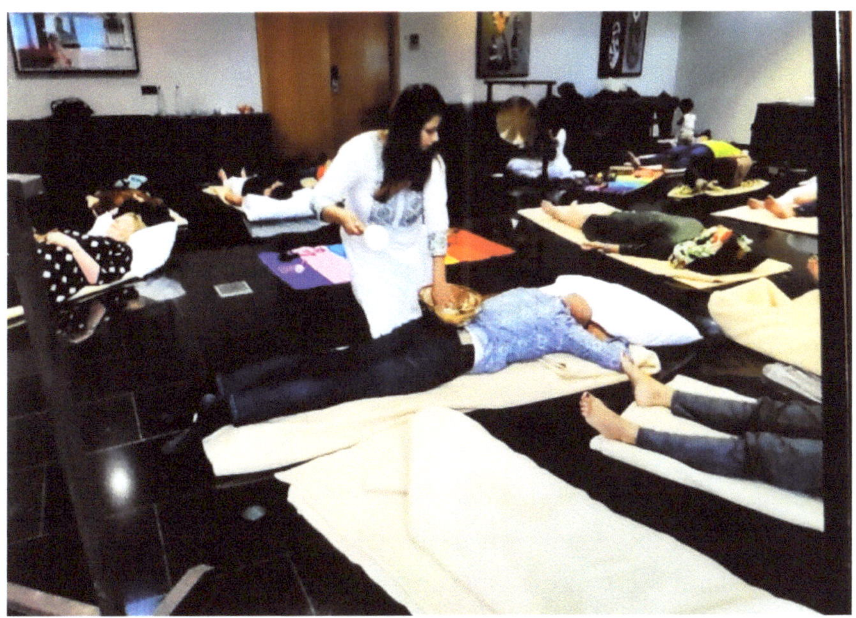

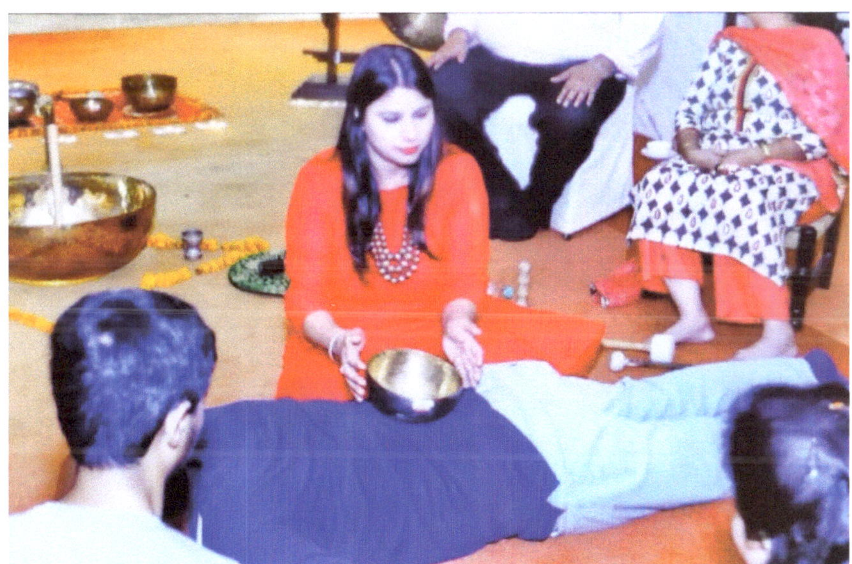

Process and Preparation

In this therapy, the patient is made to lie down comfortably. With the help of the mallet, the target pain area is first figured, and then the hot water bowl is placed on that point. It is important the patient feels the heat.

Sometimes the therapist feels the heat but the patient doesn't feel anything. For the therapy to be successful, the temperature of the water according to the patient has to be maintained. The same holds true for cold press therapy too; the patient should be able to tolerate the coldness of the bowl. This therapy takes 25 to 30 minutes.

A minimum of six sessions are mandatory to reduce the pain from the root. However, just in two or three sessions, one can find the difference in the pain as it would have started to reduce.

4.3 Chakra Healing Sound Therapy

Chakra is a Sanskrit word that denotes circle and movement. In the body, there is constant movement, which is cyclical. Chakra also means a wheel. The connection between the gross and the subtle in the human organism is through an intermediate conductor.

Before understanding this therapy, we need to understand the basis of chakras. We have seven chakras in the body. Chakras are subtle psychic centres in the body that are not seen but only perceived.

Different Types of Chakras:

There are seven chakras having seven different colours and different frequencies.

1. ROOT CHAKRA

- It deals with the basic survival instinct and is blocked by fear.
- It is represented by the colour RED.
- The element is EARTH.
- The sound to meditate is LAM.
- The Sanskrit name is MOOLADHARA CHAKRA.
- **Specific areas of healing**: Genital issues, sexual or fertility problems, rigidity, isolation, joint problems, dehydration, anything related to digestion, constipation, and fear.
- **Root chakra sound healing:** The first chakra which is at the base of the spine is the foundation of the entire chakra system. It is the ground that supports and protects you. The balancing of this chakra helps you to get more connected with mother earth. With the help of the **F** bowl or root chakra bowl, we can help and repair certain areas of the body by working on the deficiency or the excessive malfunction of the chakra by balancing them.
- **Location of chakra:** Base of spine, perineum.

2. SACRAL CHAKRA

- It deals with pleasure and is blocked by guilt.
- The colour is ORANGE.
- The element is WATER.
- Sound to meditate is VAM.
- The Sanskrit name is SWADHISTHANA CHAKRA.
- **Specific areas of healing:** Issues related to fertility, creativity, hormonal issues, sexual, fertility issues, kidney problems, low self-esteem, digestion, feeling worthless, depression, inflammation of the body, and obesity.
- **Sacral chakra sound healing:** This chakra is associated with sexual and creative energy and emotions. With the help of the **C** sound bowl or sacral chakra bowl, we can work on the specific area or issues and increase our strength, confidence, willpower, charisma, etc.
- **Location of chakra:** Lower abdomen, genital.

3. SOLAR PLEXUS CHAKRA

- It deals with willpower and is blocked by shame.
- The colour is YELLOW.
- The element is FIRE.
- Sound to meditate is RAM.
- The Sanskrit name is MANIPURA CHAKRA.
- **Specific areas of healing:** liver, kidney, diabetes, ulcer, hypoglycaemia, acidity, anxiety, gastric problems, etc.
- **Solar plexus chakra sound healing:** This chakra is associated with issues of personal power, emotions, and passion for living. With the help of the **G** bowl or solar plexus chakra sound bowl, we work on the specific area and increase willpower, compassion, and trust. The main focus of the chakra is power and identity.
- **Location of chakra:** Navel to the root of the breast.

4. HEART CHAKRA

- Deals with love and is blocked by grief and sadness.
- The colour is GREEN.
- The element is AIR.
- Sound to meditate is YAM.
- The Sanskrit name is ANAHATA CHAKRA.
- **Specific areas of healing:** Asthma, respiratory problems, heart issues, blood pressure, lung problems, immunity disorder, feeling of loneliness, depression, sadness, bipolarity, etc.
- **Heart chakra sound healing:** A balanced heart chakra opens us to love and care. When we have a balanced heart chakra, we are more open to accepting and giving. We can let go and release all the depressing energy. With the help of the **D** sound bowl or heart chakra bowl, we can work on a specific area to increase purpose, expression, compassion, love, trust, and hearing.
- **Location:** Heart centre.
- This chakra emphasises the right to love.

5. THROAT CHAKRA

- It deals with the truth and is blocked by lies.
- The colour is BLUE.
- The element is SPACE (ETHER).
- Sound to meditate is HUM.
- The Sanskrit name is VISSUDHI CHAKRA.
- **Specific areas of healing**: Thyroid, respiratory problems, bronchitis, fear of speaking, stiff neck, cervical problems, shoulder pain, blood pressure-related issues, lack of confidence, suppression of thoughts, thyroid, sinus, and throat issues.
- **Throat chakra sound healing:** when this chakra is in balance there is clear communication, and the person speaks the truth and lives creatively. With the help of the **A** sound bowl or throat chakra sound bowl, we strike the mallet to turn the suppression of thoughts into an expression of thoughts. It helps to increase understanding and also to communicate our thought in full confidence. It increases the confidence in the personality which helps in enhancing the speaking skills. This chakra helps us with the right to express ourselves.
- **Location of chakra:** Throat area.

6. THIRD-EYE CHAKRA

- It deals with insight and is blocked by illusion.
- The colour is INDIGO.
- The element is SPACE (LIGHT).
- Sound to meditate is OM.
- The Sanskrit name is AJNA CHAKRA.
- **Specific areas of healing:** Alzheimer's, confusion, mental illusion, depression, learning disability, boredom, and eye issues.
- **Third-eye chakra sound healing:** This is the gate of wisdom, and is the source of light and illumination. It enables one to gain conscious living with focus and clarity. With the help of the **E** sound bowl or third eye sound bowl, we do sound healing. In healing this chakra, the bowl is placed just above the brow or sometimes on the side of the head. It gives a very calming and relaxing effect to the body and increases wisdom, awareness, intelligence, and gives bliss. This chakra healing helps to perceive.
- **Location of chakra:** Brow centre.

7. CROWN CHAKRA

- Deals with the cosmic energy and are blocked by ego attachment.
- The colour is VIOLET.
- The element is SPACE (Thought)
- Sound to meditate is AUM.
- The Sanskrit name is SAHASTRAHARA CHAKRA.
- **Specific areas of healing:** All the connecting problems, either with the external or internal world, detachment, confusion, and not having clarity.
- **Crown chakra sound healing:** The connection of the self to the universe. It is the most subtle healing of sound as it connects the person with their own being and the true self. It is the connection between the self and divinity. With the help of the **B** sound bowl, we can build the lost connection of our mind, body, and soul. It renders the right to connect.
- **Location of chakra:** Top of the head.

  Chakra balancing and energized chakra can help us to repair and regrow the cell and the specific area by using a certain specific sound bowl. Also, sound healing can slowly create awareness of the problem in the body.

As the vibration travels through the bowl, it creates pressure and shakes the cells to get healed. This process not only helps us to find out the actual problem but also helps us to locate the complete area of the problem. It also helps to build the connection between the physiological as well as psychological aspects of the body.

When the flow of energy starts through vibration it helps the blocked energy to flow and clean the passage with the pure conscious awareness energy. This is how chakra sound healing therapy works and heals the entire body.

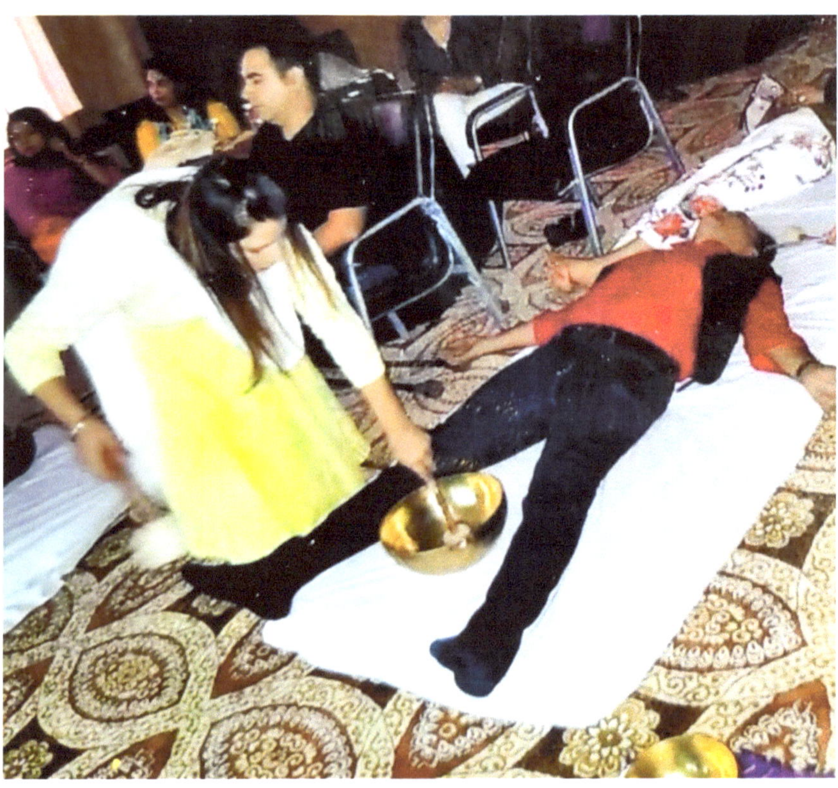

4.4 Seven Chakra Healing by Quartz Crystal Bowl

Every cell in the human body has a geometric crystalline structure. This helps our body resonate with the frequencies of quartz crystals because a quartz crystal bowl can align with your chakras. They are widely used and considered to be effective singing bowls. They can also produce the purest sounds, which can be ideal for meditation and singing bowl healing.

Clear quartz singing bowls contain seven rainbow colours which stimulate the seven energy frequencies or energy centres or chakras of your body. This helps heal by transferring pure light into the human aura. This process also expands the awareness and brings a positive shift in the consciousness of the patient. It is also believed that quartz crystals can balance the electromagnetic field of the patient during singing bowl meditation.

4.5 Sound Bath Meditation

Sound bath meditation is the sound healing session where we use a lot of higher and lower vibrations of frequency in such a manner that the vibration can be given to a large group of people at the same time.

During this meditation process, patients lie on the floor and the bowls and other musical instruments are placed in different places, either on your body or in different locations around the room.

To create sound with the singing bowl the accompanying mallets are pressed in a circular motion against the bowl's outside edges or rim. When you hear a bright clear tone you can slow down the motion; use the full arm to make the motion rather than just rotating the mallet.

Sound bath meditation combines instruments like gongs, tuning forks, Himalayan singing bowls, flutes, drums, rattles, etc. and plays the combination in such a way so that it gives maximum effect to the individual who is taking the bath. The sound vibrations from the musical bath help the individual to heal, repair, and grow beautifully. Sound bath involves pulsing sounds, clapping, drumming, and singing for ceremonial spiritual and health purposes.

4.6 Sound Music Capsule

Sound healing works by sending sound waves throughout your body which brings harmony through oscillation and resonance. It helps to restore your body balance which in turn helps you to heal. Sound healing also helps to create awareness about cells which are in a rigid form closed for years.

So, why sound music capsule?

The MORNING STANDARD

LEISURE

HEAL WITH WATER

We recommend people listen to the piece three times a day. We are creating these pieces to help people vent out their emotions which they have been holding on to for years

members, but this song was filmed with only four members Sujata Gauri, Nishi Gill, Urvashi Raman and Sharma, in Dehradun. The video was shot near a waterfall and river to complement the essence of the group's ideology. Various instruments were used: rainstick, bamboo rainstick, ocean drum, crystal bowl and a very high resonance of gong.

"Every day we take in thousands of thoughts that travel in our body. Our body has trillions of cells and our thoughts affect these cells. The after effects emerge in physical forms like cyst, tumour or clot or some kind of bigger disease. If we are uncomfortable with a particular thought, then that is affecting our body. You cannot control your surroundings, but whatev-

As we all know that capsules provide instant relief; similarly, music capsules are those capsules which provide instant relief through our ears. Sound-created problems are best healed by sound. When problems enter through the medium of vibration in the form of sound inside your body, then they should be healed through sound vibrations only. So music capsules are in the form of sound vibrations given to your ear to heal that particular toxic sound which troubles your cells and is inside your body.

Two music capsules have already been made by our musical band, the Sound of Infinity Band, which deals in healing sleep disorders. The healing properties of music capsules can help your physical and mental health. Music capsule helps in the visual as they release different hormone and neurochemical, which helps in repairing and regenerating the cells. If we listen to the music capsule twice a day or continuously for 21 to 45 days (20 to 30 min per day) we can see visible changes in our personality internally as well as externally.

4.7 Understanding of Sound and Music

The human body is designed to be exquisitely sensitive to sound. Our ability to hear developed as an 18-week foetus, making it one of the earliest senses that developed.

Research shows at the end of the second trimester a foetus responds specifically to the sound of a mother's voice.

This shows that hearing is one of our first modes of connection.

Vibrations can travel through our skin as well as the fluid and bone within us; which is why sometimes our entire body shakes receptive to sound vibration.

एशिया का पहला म्यूजिकल हीलिंग बैंड

पांच हजार साल पुरानी चिकित्सा पद्धति है साउंड हीलिंग थैरेपी: डॉ. अंजू

जयपुर आई एक्सपर्ट डॉ. अंजू शर्मा

पत्रिका PLUS रिपोर्टर

जयपुर • भागदौड़ भरी जिंदगी के बीच अपने फिजिकल और मेंटल हेल्थ को बनाए रखने के लिए साउंड वेव का इस्तेमाल किया जाने लगा है। साउंड बाउल हीलिंग थैरेपी के जरिए हम फिजिकल, मेंटल और इमोशनल हेल्थ में सुधार ला सकते हैं। अलग अलग मेटल से तैयार विशेष बाउल और उनकी साउंड का हमारी कई मेडिकल प्रॉब्लम्स को ठीक कर सकती है। यह कहना है एक्सपर्ट डॉ. अंजू शर्मा का। जयपुर आई डॉ. अंजू ने कहा कि यह थैरेपी भारत की पांच हजार साल से भी पुरानी चिकित्सा पद्धति है। एक विशेष तरह के म्यूजिक के जरिए हीलिंग या शांति का अनुभव करना ही यह थैरेपी माना जाता है।

वाइब्रेशन और फ्रिक्वेंसी पर वर्क

उन्होंने बताया कि यह तकनीक वाइब्रेशन और फ्रिक्वेंसी पर काम करती है। हमारे शरीर के सेल्स में ये वाइब्रेशन पहुंचती हैं और उन समस्याओं को दूर करती हैं, जिससे हम परेशान हैं। इस थैरेपी में साउंड बाउल के साथ दूसरे साउंड्स का भी इस्तेमाल किया जाता है, जिससे व्यक्ति में मौजूद नेगेटिव एनर्जी के अलावा दूसरी प्रॉब्लम्स को भी ठीक किया जा सके। इसमें आत्म शांति के लिए 'ओम' साउंड, नेगेटिव एनर्जी को खत्म करने और घर का वातावरण शुद्ध करने के लिए विंड चाइम साउंड का प्रयोग किया जाता है। वहीं योगा, मेडिटेशन शुरू करने और खत्म करते वक्त सिंगिंग बाउल साउंड, दिमागी और शारीरिक शांति के लिए तिंगशा साउंड व मन में चेतना जाग्रत करने के लिए डोर्जे मेडिटेशन बेल साउंड का इस्तेमाल किया जाता है।

बैंड में 11 मेम्बर

डॉ. अंजू ने बताया कि साउंड वाइब्रेशन के बारे में ज्यादा से ज्यादा लोगों को बताने के लिए हमने एशिया का पहला म्यूजिकल हीलिंग बैंड बनाया है, इसकी लॉन्चिंग दिसम्बर में हुई है। अब हम देशभर में अलग अलग जगहों पर कॉन्सर्ट प्लान कर रहे हैं। बैंड के जरिए हम लोगों को म्यूजिकल हीलिंग से ठीक करते हैं। हमारे बैंड में 11 मेंबर हैं जो 14 अलग अलग इंस्ट्रूमेंट्स पर काम करते हैं।

The concept of understanding music as therapy would not exist without sound. Everything musical is made from sound. And yet the reverse is not true. There are many sounds which are not musical.

Musical sound or any tone with characteristics such as controlled pitch and timbre are produced by instruments in which the periodic vibrations can be controlled by the performer.

The vibrations which produce a harmonious effect and are in rhythm are musical sounds. Just like the mantras we chant, like OM, it's harmonious.

More like, chanting of mantras, affirmations, quotes, songs, poems, anything which flows in pattern in rhythm brings our body in harmony and is musical to our ears.

So we can say that we create "sound out of sound."

05

TOOLS AND INSTRUMENTS USED IN SOUND HEALING

5.1 Tibetan Healing Bowl

Tibetan singing bowls are used for deep relaxation and muscle regeneration to relieve pain in joints muscles and shoulders, to ease pain related to sciatica, the digestive system, headache and migraine, or spine injury, and to improve circulation by releasing tension.

How to use healing bowls?

Hold the bowl in the palm of your non-dominating hand and the mallet in your dominating hand, hold the mallet like a baton and lightly strike the bowl's mid-exterior wall.

Tibetan healing sound bowls are specially designed in a way to give proper healing to the cells, which are rigid and tense. These bowls are specially made on full moon nights and with nine metals. Both machine-made and handmade healing bowls are used for sound healing therapy.

5.2 Himalayan Singing Bowl

These bowls are generally made from a bronze alloy containing copper, tin, zinc, iron, lead, silver, gold, and nickel. It is a type of standing bowl played by striking or rubbing its rim with a wooden or leather-wrapped mallet. This excitation causes the sides and rim of the bowl to vibrate producing a rich sound.

Buddhist monks have long used singing bowls in meditation practice. Some wellness practitioners including music therapists, masseurs, and yoga therapists also use these singing bowls during treatment.

5.3 Crystal Singing Bowl

Crystal singing bowls are made up of pure quartz (essentially 99.8% silicon quartz) which is heated and crushed under high temperature and made into different bowls.

Crystal bowls are clear and frosted and are made in a variety of sizes ranging from five to 24 inches clear. Crystal bowls are generally lighter, and smaller and can be played by holding in hand. During the manufacturing process crystal bowl can be created to a specific frequency and tuned to produce a specific sound depending on individual needs.

5.4 Gong

The Chinese used gongs for many ceremonial functions. They were struck to announce when the emperor or other important political or religious figure arrived. Military leaders also used gong to gather men for battle.

Gong is made up of nine metals and it looks like a plate hung on a stand. Gong is further divided into three types:

- **The suspended gong** is a flat circular disc with holes near the top of its outer circumference.

- **Nipple gong is** also known as a bossed gong. These gongs feature a raised boss or knob in the middle of a metal disc.

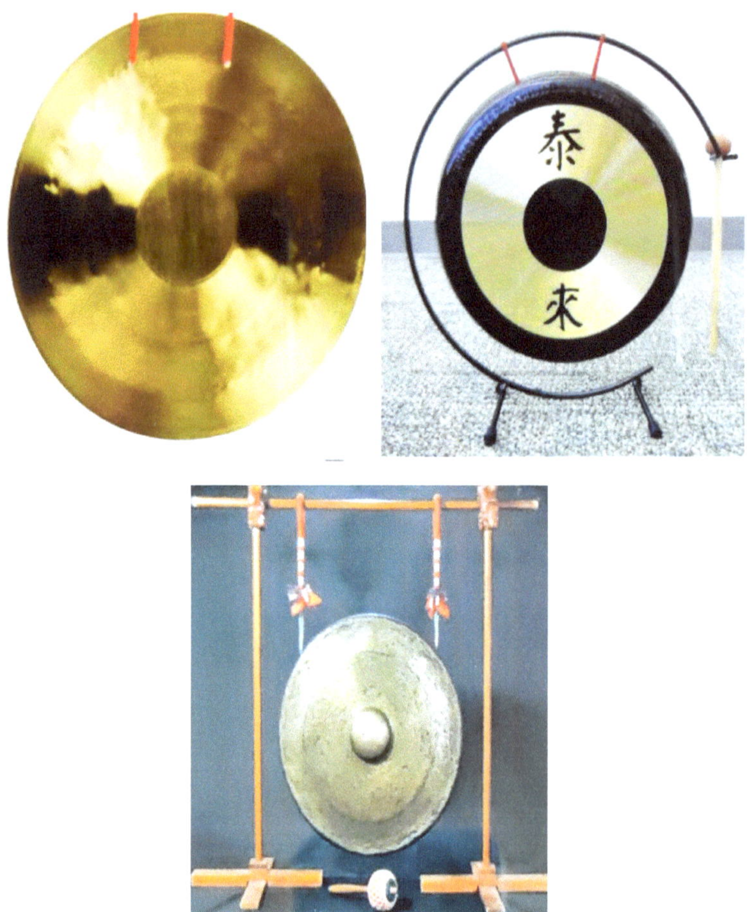

- **Bowl Gong** These musical instruments are also known as singing bowls.

Sound is produced either by striking the gong or rubbing it with the mallet. There are different kinds of mallets for the gong. The gong is struck in the centre, on the knob, since it is here that the greatest volume and purest tone are produced.

Gong is considered the God of sound in ancient times. Sixteen different types of sounds come through the gong to heal the people in a different pattern.

5.5 Xylophone

The xylophone has been used for purposes other than music. The type of wood used to create the bars of the xylophone can result in different sounds.

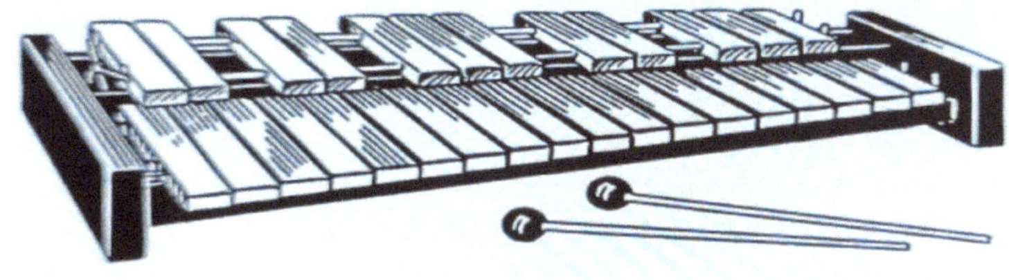

It is a wooden percussion instrument with a range of four octaves and can be used in a variety of musical genres. Although they are present in the traditional music of Africa, Europe, Southeast Asia and more, their birthplace remains a mystery.

5.6 Hapi Drum

The unique tone of the Hapi drum is created by a tuned vibrating tongue of steel. The concept is similar to a wooden tongue drum. When a tongue is quickly and lightly struck with the finger or mallet its vibration creates sound waves.

5.7 Hand Pan

Hand pan is now the most common term to qualify hand-like instruments. It was coined by Kyle Cox at Pantheon Steel. Unlike the steel drum, hand pans are played by hand. It emerged as an alternative to the trademark Hang.

It is a beautiful instrument that can correspond to the frequencies of all the chakras if played in a pattern. It gives a relaxing effect on the mind, body, and soul.

5.8 Singing Bell and Vajra

It consists of a heavily decorated bell metal bronze hand bell (the ghanta) and a decorated bell metal bronze sceptre

It is known as the Dorje or Vajra. Only the bell makes a sound although both instruments are always used together in sound healing because, in Tibetan Buddhism, they symbolize the sacred masculine and feminine

The practitioner uses the bell to move and break up or harmonize life force energy by striking it with a mallet.

Sound is produced by running the mallet around the rim of the Dorje or Vajra, which is then placed on the body in different ways to facilitate the energy flow, while the practitioner works with the bell.

5.9 Ocean Drum

An ocean drum is a double-sided drum filled with small metal beats, which produce a nice relaxing and mellow sound of waves when moved around.

By increasing or decreasing the speed of the movement, one can produce sounds of gentle waves or crashing waves. The sound coming from ocean drums makes you feel like you are sitting near the ocean. This instrument is very powerful in clearing the water element of the body and is also useful in meditation.

5.10 Rain stick

The rain stick is used to create atmospheric sounds and as a percussion instrument. The rain stick is generally used to create the sound effect of rain or when shaken a sound similar to the maracas is produced.

Rain stick is made up of special wood, designed in a way that it produces the sound of rain droplets when shaken properly. There are different kinds of shapes and sizes of rain sticks, which plays a vital role in healing the cells of the body.

5.11 Wind Chimes

Wind chimes are used not just for their sound effects but also for purifying and enhancing energy within a certain area. A mark tree (also known as a nail tree, charm tree, or set of bar chimes) is a percussion instrument used primarily for musical colour.

It consists of many small chimes, which are typically cylinders of solid aluminium or hollow brass tubes 3/8" in diameter of a variety of lengths mounted hanging from a bar.

Wind chimes are also used in Feng Shui to enhance the energy of the house. The sound coming from the wind chimes give a pleasing effect to your heart chakra and cleanses the energy of the house.

5.12 Tuning Fork

A tuning fork is a metal fork that can be used as an acoustic resonator. Traditionally, this tool has been used to tune musical instruments. Tuning forks work by releasing a perfect wave pattern to match a musician's instrument.

In the medical profession, tuning forks remain a preferred method of testing for certain types of hearing loss. Testing for hearing loss with a tuning fork is called a Rinne test. If X-rays are in short supply, doctors will use a tuning fork to identify whether a bone is fractured or not. A tuning fork in sound healing gives a certain amount of vibrations to targeted cells and helps reduce the rigidity and tension of the cell, which helps the body to get into an ease condition.

5.13 Kalimba

Kalimba or Mbira (or many other names) is also known as the thumb piano. It is an instrument that originated in Africa.

It is a member of the idiophone family, meaning that it is an instrument whose sound is produced primarily by vibration without the use of strength or membranes.

The kalimba features the seven-note diatonic scale, used in traditional Western music while the non-Western scale of the kalimba features the same note but not in the same order.

Kalimba produces a pleasant sound played in a pattern that helps in calming your body. It also comes in different sizes.

5.14 Flute

The flute is a family of musical instruments in the woodwind group. Unlike woodwind instruments with reeds, a flute is a narrow reed-less wind instrument that produces sound from the flow of air across an opening. It works on the mechanism of air. Also, it helps to balance the air element of the body. There are many types of flutes but the main work of flutes is to give harmony to the heart chakra and give a balance to the flow of energy in the body.

5.15 Crystal Pyramid

Crystal pyramids are made from over 99.9% pure quartz crystal, a naturally occurring element. Crystal singing pyramid is a kind of musical instrument that can be used for treatment to clarify the mind to achieve a state of deep meditation.

Crystal pyramids are made up of a rod of quartz in a pyramid shape. It is used by placing it on the head of the people who are taking the therapy.

The crystal pyramid works on the three-dimension energy:

- Physical dimension
- Mental dimension
- Emotional dimension

All these instruments used in sound healing therapy are very powerful instruments as they not only give relaxation to the body but also work on the deep traumas of the body and help the body to rise and shine.

06

RELEVANCE OF SOUND HEALING

6.1 Importance of Sound Healing

As sound healing therapy is very powerful it works from the micro to macro level.

Some of the possible uses and importance includes:

- **Stress relief**: some research supports the use of Tibetan singing bowls as a way to promote relaxation and reduce the feeling of anxiety.
- **Improves sleep**: Singing bowl therapy has been linked to decreasing anxiety and tension it may help improve sleep.
- **Lowering blood pressure**: A preliminary study published in the American Journal of Health in 2014, examined the benefits of starting a directed relaxation session with 12 minutes of the singing bowl and found a greater reduction in systolic blood pressure and heart rate compared to silence before the session.
- **Reducing depression**: One study linked singing bowl therapy to improvement in mood as a low-cost way to reduce symptoms of depression as it breaks the tension in the cells and relaxes them.
- **Stimulating the immune system**: It can stimulate the immune system and produce beneficial changes in brain waves. It helps relax and calm the waves of the cells which helps in repairing the cells and aids in the brain growth.
- **Balancing and harmonizing the body**: The vibrations of the therapy can produce beneficial changes in the body by harmonizing the cell and balancing the body's energy system. As the vibration

comes through to the bowl, it tunes the water molecule so that each cell synchronizes in a harmonious rhythm. It also harmonizes our hormones.

- **Pain relief**: It helps in reducing pain by calming the cells and reducing stress at the cell level. Once the pain area is identified, sound therapy is used to release the pain in the cells.
- **Enhancing other healing practices**: Some people use sound therapy bowls in meditation and combine them with other healing practices such as deep breathing, singing and also in yoga. In ancient times yoga included sounds in the form of *nadayoga*.
- **Helps in mood swing**: It helps in changing the moods, especially calm downs impulsive behaviour and brings the body into a soothing effect.

During the pandemic times, sound therapy has played a vital role in reducing mental stress and mental blockages to bring the body into its most ease form for many people.

6.2 How Sound Healing Helps Physiological as Well as Psychological Wellbeing

Any problem which we see in our life either physical or psychological enter inside our body through five sensory organs—eyes, ears, nose, mouth, skin and most important through the sixth sense which is our thought.

The thoughts enter our body in the form of vibrations; these vibrations can travel through visual, auditory, and kinaesthetic senses depending upon the sensory organ prominently used.

The vibration travels through the ears and reaches the brain through the auditory nerves where the message is transferred to the entire body. These vibrations are stored in the cells and block our mental health which later if not treated can affect our physical health too. Every problem which enters our body is mainly through the vibrational mode and through which our body acts accordingly. So sound healing helps a body to release that vibration which is blocked in the cell, or passage of information which we receive through the medium of vision, auditory, kinaesthetic and block that passage to release the information. Sound healing vibration not only relaxes but also removes and cleanses the passage of that toxic information which makes our cells uncomfortable.

Any problem inside the body that disturbs our cells enter through the sensory organs. So first if we need to work on physical and psychological behaviour we have to see the vibrational information coming inside our body in the form of emotions.

EMOTION = E + MOTION
Where E = ENERGY
M = MOTION (Movement)

Any energy which is blocking or not moving become emotional blockage. And also bring ourselves into un-ease condition. This is the main reason for our diseases, either physical, mental, or emotional.

There is a constant movement of energy or vibrations between the external atmosphere and the inside of our bodies. When our body resists the free flow of movement it results in a dis-ease condition. This also results in an emotional block, which affects the cells. So, sound healing works on the first layer which is vibrations entering your body, repairing the cells slowly. Also during the therapy, the person can understand the mechanism of their body and also becomes aware of the information that is the vibrations or thoughts coming inside the body; he can understand which information is disturbing him or making his body into an unease condition.

So here we can say:

EMOTIONAL HEALTH AFFECTS – MENTAL HEALTH AFFECTS – PHYSICAL HEALTH

So sound healing works on these three levels simultaneously first on the emotional health (**vibrational level)** then on mental health (**psychological level)** then on the physical **(physiological level).**

Also, it creates awareness regarding the body to grow and repair by itself.

6.3 Sound Healing in Astrology and Vastu Shastra

Everything in this universe is in vibrational frequency which we have to tune and bring together in harmony and rhythm. If the cosmic energies are in the rhythm of the individual the external and internal environment of a being will be in tune and harmony. So to bring harmony to your body you need to bring the external environment also in harmony.

But normally it's not the case because of our current lifestyle and the daily routine not only our bodies but also the cosmic vibrations of the universe. All of us are a part of this universe so it is very important to bring our bodies into the rhythm of the cosmic vibration.

Nine is a very significant number: there are nine frequencies, nine directions, nine planets, and nine colours in this universe. So everything in this universe revolves around figure nine. So the correct rhythm of the cosmic vibration should be within nine; anything that goes beyond nine will cause a non-harmonious effect.

COLOUR	CHAKRA	FREQUENCY
VIOLET	CROWN	768 Hz
INDIGO	THIRD EYE	720 Hz
BLUE	THROAT	672 Hz
GREEN	HEART	594 Hz
YELLOW	SOLAR PLEXUS	582 Hz
ORANGE	SACRAL	480 Hz
RED	ROOT	432 Hz

White and black are two more colours that are equally important as white comes after violet and reflect all the frequencies and black absorbs all the frequencies.

- Nine Planets: Mercury, Venus, Earth, Mars, Jupiter, Saturn, Uranus, Neptune, Pluto

- Nine Directions: East (E), west (W), north (N), south (S), north-east (NE), north-west (NW), south-east (SE), south-west (SW), and the centre of the house (Brahmasthan; B).

Sound healing helps to bring all the frequencies into their original state and position. Sound healing creates vibrations in the planet and directions. Sometimes it produces hyper-vibration (too many vibrations) and sometimes hypo vibration (very less vibration). It is important to bring a balance between the two so that we can bring the cosmic energies into harmony.

Due to the vibrational effects planet become deficient or efficient which can cause planetary effects. It is for the same reason, that people wear gems stones of different colours which signifies the vibrations the stone brings to the person.

Similarly with the direction sometimes some directions emit extra energy and sometimes some directions become weak. So, sound healing therapy balances it by producing some sound in that direction in the home. The special kind of sound healing which is called *dhauniyagya* has been done to produce the vibration for maintaining the harmony of all the directions and bringing them in a balance.

So, we can say that sound healing therapy is a divine therapy because it not only balances and tunes our body with ourselves but also tunes our body to cosmic energy.

As clearly mentioned in the previous chapters we have seen the *beej mantra* for each chakra. So we can also harmonize our chakra and frequencies and the associated planet, directions, colours, and elements by chanting those *beej* mantras.

A quick recap:

- Root chakra: LAM, nose: smell
- Sacral chakra: VAM, tongue: taste
- Solar plexus: RAM, eyes: sight
- Heart chakra: YAM, skin: touch
- Throat chakra: HAM, ears: hearing
- Third-eye chakra: OM, connection
- Crown chakra: AUM, silence.

Continuous practise of these *beej* mantras focusing on the area given above and with the sensory organ will help you to regulate and stimulate the awareness of the related organ. This will help you to get healed and repair your body not only physically, psychologically, emotionally, but cosmically and spiritually too.

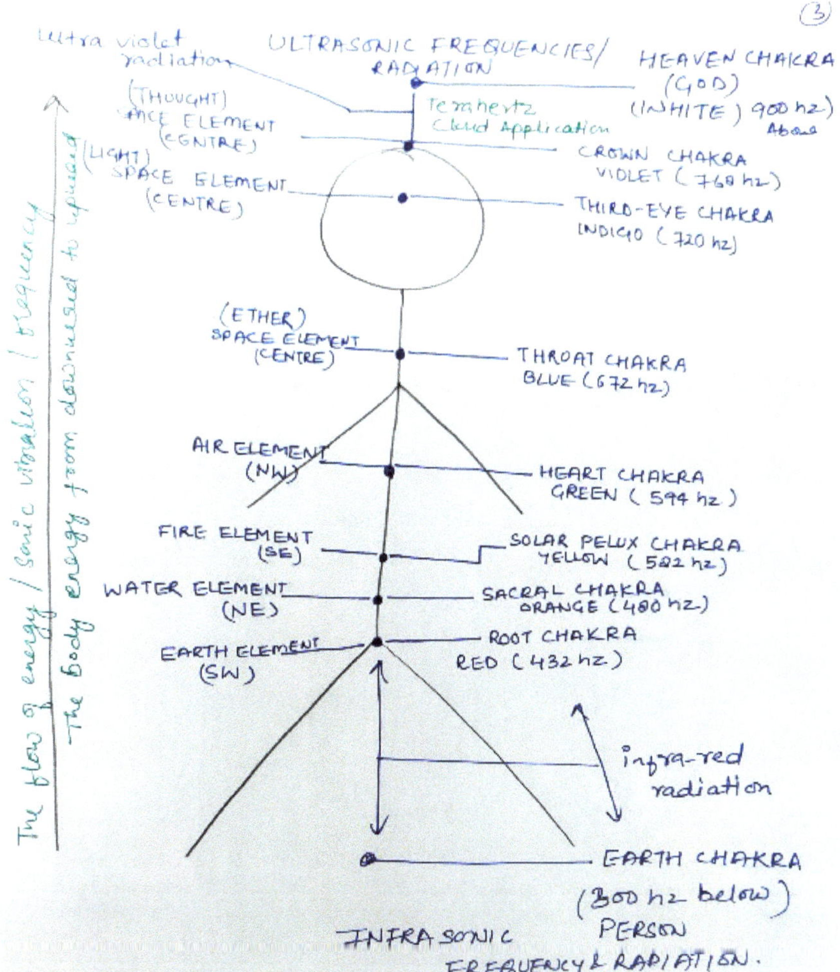

DIAGRAMATIC RERRESENTATION OF COSMOLOGY, PHYSIOLOGY PSYCHOLOGY & SPIRITUAL CONNECTION OF UNIVERSE WITH HUMAN.

07

RESEARCH INCLUDES SOME CASE STUDIES

Case Study 1: Skin Allergy

Problem: Skin allergy, especially on the face, pimples, small spots with inflammation, and itching on the face.

- Name**:** Mrs Rakhi Handa
- Age: 27
- Place**:** Ludhiana, Punjab
- Gender: Female
- Problem: Allergy on the face
- Therapy given: Sound brain wave therapy, along with water meditation therapy.
- Number of sessions: 7
- **Mode of treatment**:

  Findings: The first step is to understand the problem of the patient, who had inflammation on both sides of her face near the cheek area. The swelling and redness around the cheek were visible. During the counselling sessions, it became clear that the patient was unable to express her thoughts verbally and she was quite depressed.

  Her allergies were mostly concentrated around the cheek area and on the side of the forehead; this indicates that she has some thoughts which she was not able to share, and now that particular thought has heated up and the area was filled with water. This normally happens when the patient is under healing crises or in hanging healing. So now the inflammation and redness are visible. Her problem was from her childhood she believed that she was not intelligent enough or responsible enough to handle anything in her life. But when people started to appreciate and believed in her, her body started the reverse psychological pattern because she was not used to hearing good comments, therefore her body came under hanging healing, which resulted in inflammation, causing swelling and itching and redness between the area of her ears and mouth that is cheeks.

So here **sound brain wave therapy** worked magic for her. We used three sound healing bowls—crown chakra sound healing bowl, third eye chakra sound healing bowl, and throat chakra sound healing bowl.

Method: First we placed the bowls around the patient's head. Then using a mallet we started the intensity according to the itching intensity of the inflammation of cells. Performing this therapy continuously for 10 to 15 minutes relaxed and calmed the patient. In two sessions, her inflammation and redness had gone and the spots began to fade. By the fourth session, the spots become invisible. After four sessions of brain wave sound therapy, we added water meditation for the patient to listen to at her home, at least twice a day for a week.

Within five sessions, a visible change was seen. Her itching, allergy symptoms and pimples were reduced by 82—85%. Over the following weeks, she is absolutely fine with glowing skin without any spots.

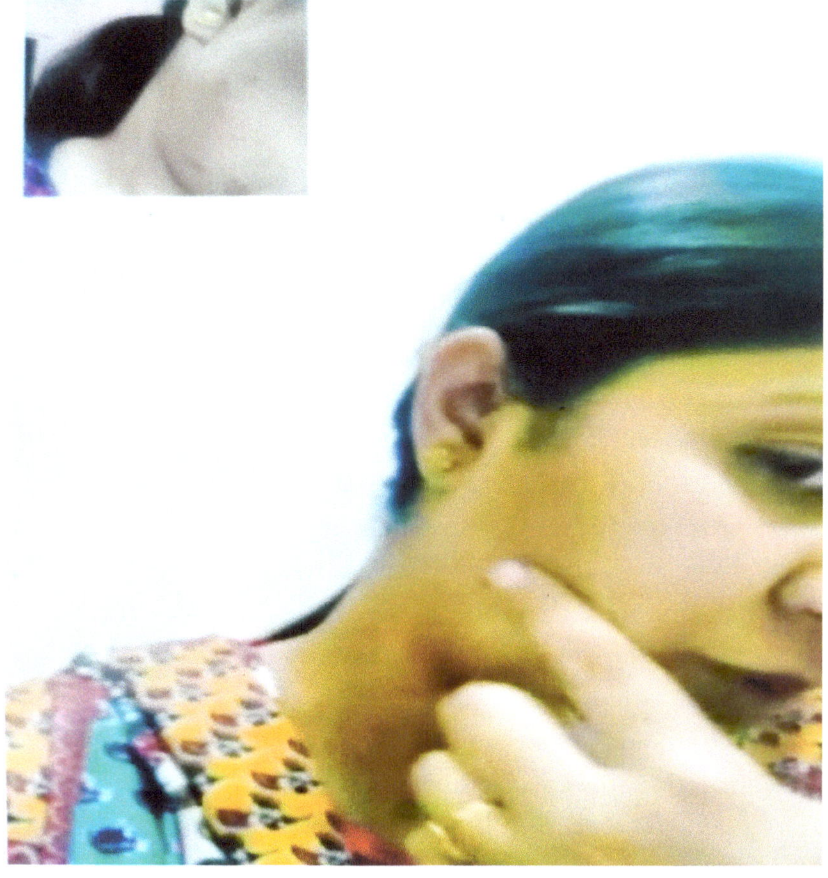

Rakhi Handa: The case of inflammation, itching, and allergy spots was cured by brain wave sound healing therapy.

Case Study 2: Hyper Anxiety with Impulsive Behaviour

Problem: Hyper anxiety with impulsive behaviour

- Name: Mrs Parul
- Age: 35
- Place: Punjab
- Gender: Female
- Problem: Anxiety, aggressive behaviour, suppression
- Therapy given: Water sound meditation along with colour therapy, counselling session, and anger management sound therapy.
- Number of sessions: 6
- **Mode of treatment**:
- **Findings**: This is a case of aggressive behaviour, recorded aggression, sadness, symptoms of manic and shows an impulsive reaction. During the counselling sessions, it was understood that the patient had lost her younger brother in COVID 19, and she was not able to cope with this incident. This trauma led to a deep suppression of emotions which later turned into hyper-aggressive behaviour towards her family.

  So, we worked with her using **trauma-releasing sound therapy**. In subsequent sessions, we gradually brought her to move from suppressing her emotions to expressing them. During those sessions, the patient was able to express many long-suppressed emotions from her young age too. So the trauma was not just the death of her brother, which was but a trigger of maximum intensity that brought out all her young age emotional suppressions.

  Method: So we finally decided to work with **brain waves sounds** and **water meditation sound therapies.** Simultaneously, we helped her with OM meditations and chanting along with water music. After the first three sessions, the patient showed visible changes in her behaviour. She showed more restraint in her aggression. We also applied colour therapy and metaphor therapy. We continued with trauma sound healing therapy and counselled her regularly to heal her damaged and toxic thoughts. Parallelly, the water sound frequencies helped regenerate her cells from inside. The water meditation, especially, helps to repair the brain cells to promote a change in the behaviour of the patient towards her family.

Today, the patient exhibits a very calm attitude and has accepted her brother's death. She has also incorporated meditation daily in her life.

Case Study 3: Suicidal Tendency

Problem**:** Suicidal tendency

- Name: Ms Shivani Yadav
- Age: 21
- Place: Delhi
- Gender: Female
- Problem: Suicidal behaviour, random faintness, low confidence
- Therapy given: Trauma sound healing, water meditation, colour therapy, wind-chime sound
- Number of sessions: Three months
- **Mode of treatment**:
- **Findings**: This patient had already consulted many doctors and was also admitted several times to the hospital.
  In the first discussion, we figured that the girl tended to escape from her problems without facing them. She believed that nobody listens to her or understands her. Over time, her body didn't support her mind, and her mind started escaping from the issues and she had periodic fainting episodes. It was clear every time she faced a discussion that she didn't want to face or talk about, she fainted. The girl had found a defence mechanism from her problems.
  Her suicidal tendencies revealed the same, a more advanced form of escapism, that she didn't want to face any difficult situations in life. In German medicine science, we call this flying mode or skipping mode.
  Method: We used sound water therapy to make her understand that escaping her problems was not a solution in life. Through further counselling sessions, we understood that she had grown up in a house of constant sibling comparison.
  Once she became aware of the real issue, she started to speak up.
  That's a big milestone in her therapy because as soon as she started talking about her issues, within a month, her fainting episodes

stopped. We also taught her certain techniques to face a problem and express her emotions through those techniques.

The next step was to make sure that she was healed at the cell level so that in future nothing would trigger her back into a flying mode. Through the counselling sessions along with the trauma healing sessions, we worked on her deep-rooted trauma where we found a lot of things from her childhood and we worked on those points too, with the sound trauma therapy. We work with water frequencies like rain sounds, wind chimes, crystal bowls, ocean drums, and Himalayan Tibetan bowls specifically with the **F** root bowl.

Her basic problem was her insecurity and feeling abandoned. However, as soon as she became aware of the real problem, she came into a surrendering mode and then her therapy took a high speed. The cells showed rapid healing, so her physical body showed signs of improvement. The girl also became comfortable talking to her mother about her issues. She has also started attending college regularly now.

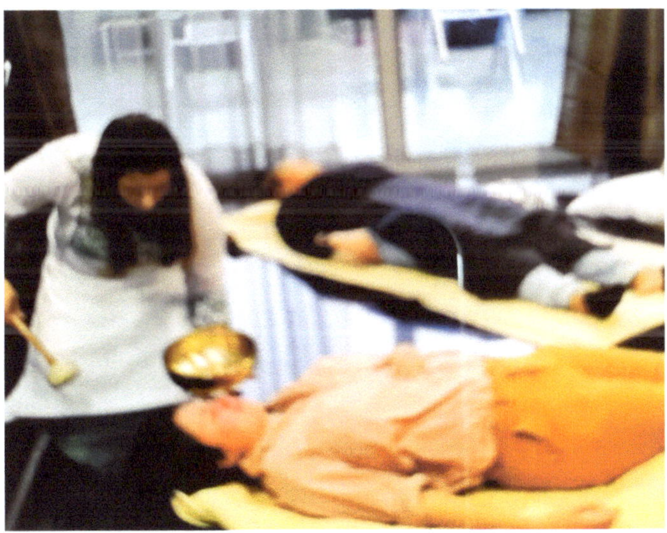

Trauma healing therapy along with guided sounds of affirmation to break the suppression.

Case Study 4: Severe UTI Infection

Problem: Severe UTI infection

- Name: Ms Monika Gupta
- Age: 24 year
- Place: Jaipur, Rajasthan
- Gender: Female
- Problem: Severe UTI infection with pain in passing urine and also pain while sitting and walking.
- Therapy given: Seven chakra sound healing therapy along with some aroma oil.
- Number of sessions: 15 days
- **Mode of treatment**:
- **Findings and method**: The patient first attended a group session. We performed **seven chakra sound healing meditations** for 30 minutes on all the participants. In the session, a **G** bowl was placed on the solar plexus and vibrations were given to each one of the individuals present.

  After the group session, this patient said that she was suffering from a severe UTI infection and was in constant pain. But after just 30 minutes of attending the chakra healing sound meditation, she admitted to feeling much better. She also asked for personal sessions to treat her UTI.

  After a few sessions, we noticed how her face and body were looking more relaxed and she said that the pain while sitting and standing was gone. Soon, she also wanted us to heal her fears and insecurity issues. For this, we used the **F** and **C** bowls which are the root chakra bowl and sacral chakra bowl.

  Along with colour therapy and sound frequencies of water we worked on her fear of finances. We also performed the therapy specifically for the inflammation and the pain in the private area which indicates the fear is related to the marriage, partner, money and sexuality. We worked on each part of her life and used sound vibrations and natural sounds like rain and advised her to sit near the water area along with some aroma oils like rose and lavender oils; after 15 days of therapy, her infection was gone completely. However, we advised her to continue her conventional medicines along with the sound therapy. Further counselling sessions revealed that she had some territorial issues that resulted in the UTI infection.

Case Study 5: Liver Cirrhosis

Problem: Liver cirrhosis

- Name: Mr Harmesh Lal Raina
- Age: 69 years
- Place: Jammu
- Gender: Male
- Problem: Liver cirrhosis, low appetite, weakness in the body.
- Therapy given: Intense trauma healing, circular detox sound therapy, aroma therapy, frequency of water & counselling
- Number of sessions: Six months
- **Mode of treatment**:
- **Findings**: Cirrhosis also called hepatitis cirrhosis indicates chronic liver damage from a variety of causes leading to scarring and liver failure.

  Mr Lal came with the problem of liver cirrhosis, severe weakness and a very low diet with other psychological issues.

  Before coming to us, he had consulted doctors from different parts of the country. All had unanimously said that his liver was very weak and his stomach was not functioning optimally. Because digestion was not proper, food intake was reduced and thus he had become weak.

  His condition also induced the fear of losing his life and he worried for his family. Because of the cost either. So along with his physiological issues, the patient was assailed by mental problems too.

  The patient thus switched to alternative therapies and found out about the *nadayoga* or sound healing therapy,

  Method: We started working on his body, specifically the area near the liver with the **G** bowl so that the guilt of the traumas which his body is suffering from can calm down.

  In the first session, we performed brain wave therapy to make his mind calm and to bring all the body cells in harmony.

In the second session, we performed counselling along with some water frequencies where the rest of the body cells was set to surrender towards the therapy.

In the third therapy, we performed a trauma healing therapy where we worked on his past trauma and current problem so that the body comes in alignment with the treatment.

Later on after a few days; we performed trauma sound therapy along with some pain relief therapies using **G**, **F**, **C**, **E**, and self-healing bowl,

During this therapy, a lot of findings were found as his body was completely in a surrendering mode and all the vibrations coming out of the sound healing bowls work in a receiving mode. This therapy goes on for nearly two and a half hours.

The therapy was performed to help the patient let go of all the emotional blockages set inside his body from childhood.

Later after continuously giving him sound frequencies along with other therapies, his body became calm and relaxed, and the patient fell asleep. When he woke up after a few hours, his face glowed and he seemed to have gotten up with renewed energy.

This process of sound healing was performed three more times.

After he went back to Jammu, he was asked to continue the process of sound chakra healing therapy and we guided him through the online medium. After one month when he got his check-up, his medical report gave a different story; the liver count was 13; when he had come to us he had 32.

Today he continues to maintain this positive lifestyle of yoga, meditation, and sound healing.

It worked miraculously for this patient because he surrendered to the therapy and worked with full willpower and determination.

He continues to eat a normal good diet and is living a good and healthy life.

His life transformation has been recorded in the life transformation series episode 4 by the Sound of Infinity Band on YouTube.

The success of this particular patient was also that he never lost hope even for a second.

Mr Harmesh Lal Raina was a true example of inspiration and determination and a true warrior.

In Conversation with Shri Harmesh Lal Raina
on his life transformation Journey

The interview of Mr Harmesh Lal Raina, sharing his journey experience on "Life transformation series by Dr Anju Sharma on Facebook/YouTube channel: https://fb.watch/9xq7nc0168/

Case Study 6: Severe Arthritis

- **Problem**: Severe Arthritis
- Name: Mrs Neelam Mishra
- Age: 42 years
- Place: Ghaziabad, Uttar Pradesh
- Gender: Female
- Problem: Severe arthritis, inflammation in joints, emotional suppression
- Therapy given: Trauma healing sound therapy, brain wave therapy, chakra balancing sound therapy, aroma therapy, colour therapy
- Number of sessions: 7
- **Mode of treatment**:
- **Findings**: This is a case of severe arthritis with lots of inflammation in joints and emotional blockage. The patient was used to taking lots of heavy doses of medicine to come out of the pain.
- **Method**: So the first mode of treatment was to perform **colour therapy** and thorough counselling to understand the root reason for arthritis. We found out that the person was suffering from issues of belongingness.

  We started work through a **trauma sound healing session** where we performed the therapy with the intense **G** solar plexus bowl and **F** root chakra bowl. With the help of these two bowls, the patient can let go of all fear, guilt, and shame stories which they are hiding inside the body.

  During the therapy, we also found that there were a lot of anxieties going on in her personal life which she was not able to express.

  While continuously working on her body, we worked on her pain and the joints.

  In the later cellular detox sound healing therapy, we worked on her cells to reduce the suppression level and decrease the suppressed thoughts set in her subconscious mind.

  While performing the therapy she continuously responded to the therapy but she was also continuously biting her teeth as she was having a lot of suppressed anger in the form of separation inside the body.

We also worked on her anger management through sound by using **brain wave therapy** and also by giving some guided meditation frequencies.

The deep state from where we started with **C, F, G** bowl and lastly with **A** bowl, induced her to express freely her thoughts. After the last therapy her face was glowing, facial expressions were changed, and her pain became less. We continued the pattern of therapy followed by some aromas and counselling sessions.

Rose oil and eucalyptus oil were advised for her heart and throat chakra to give relief to her pain and to support her emotional issues. The inflammation caused inside the body due to the water stored in the cell with the toxic thoughts was treated through the sound healing therapy, wherein we gave vibration to those cells, to help them repair, regrow and regenerate.

Later on, the therapy and the guided frequencies such as water frequency and fire frequency were given to her so that she had relief from the deep depression and the deep separation.

After a few therapies and supportive frequency given to her the tendency of her pain and the suppression of her emotions reduced, today she has become a very expressive and confident person. Now, she is a certified sound trainer who is treating other people's pain through sound therapy. She has become a true inspiration to all.

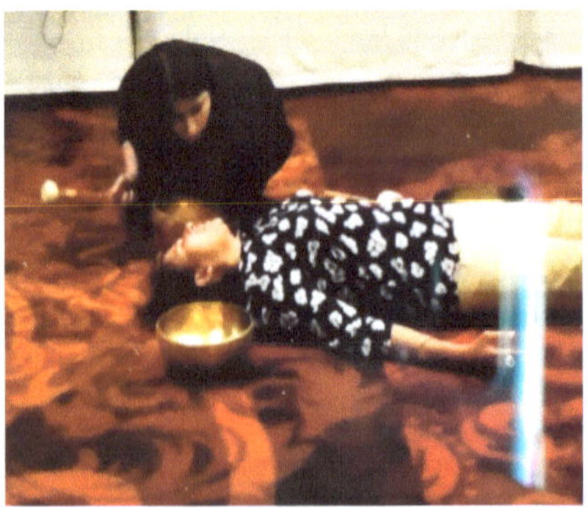

Trauma sound healing therapy on Neelam Mishra by Dr Anju Sharma

08

COMPARATIVE ANALYSIS OF SOUND HEALING

8.1 Productivity of Cells Through Sound Healing

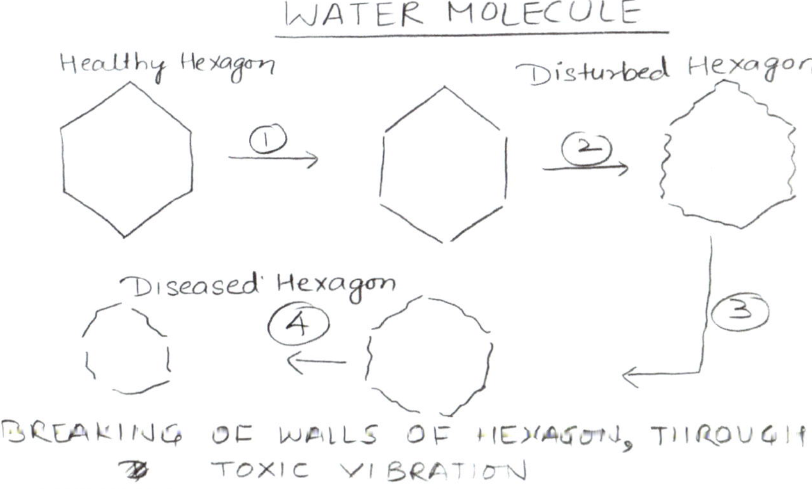

Sound healing is the healing tool which helps the individual by repairing, and regrowing cells, and creates awareness regarding both the internal and the external well-being as compared to other therapies.

Our body is made up of trillions of cells and each cell has water molecules. Also, more than 70% of our body is made up of water. So when there is an external disturbance the hexagon-shaped water molecules also get disturbed and the wall of the hexagon formula starts breaking up slowly and slowly as shown in the above figure. This causes inflammation and rigidity of cells.

Sound healing is the only healing tool that helps in repairing the wall of the water molecule (the hexagon structure) and also helps in regenerating and rejuvenating the cells.

Through the vibrations coming from the sound healing bowls, the productivity of the cell can be increased as it helps to build the wall of the hexagon in the initial stage where the cell and water molecules also (hexagon structure) are healthier.

The vibrations coming through the bowls also help repair the cells and remove the toxic vibrations which are deeply settled inside the body. Since we listen at the frequency of 20 Hz to 20000 Hz, so with the help of our auditory nerves and skin we remove all the toxic vibrations.

Sound healing not only increases the productivity of the cell but also helps us to form the original shape of the cell which increases and helps in rejuvenating life.

8.2 Increase the Efficiency of the Brain

The main aim of sound healing is to bring the body into its original form where the body is comfortable and able to live healthily.

It increases the efficiency of the system. The chakras are the energy points in the body through which we command the entire body. The auditory nerves transmit the vibrations through the energy points, reach the brain and from there are distributed to the entire body through the auto nervous system which helps to repair the cells of the body. The neurotransmitters also give the command to the entire body to build the connection between the mind and the body accordingly.

The vibrations produced through sound healing bowls repair and help regrow the passage and increase the efficiency of cells.

As the vibration travels through the auditory nerve, the electric charge reaches the auditory nerve to the fourth layer of the brain which is the cortex and through the auditory nerves of the cortex, the message is transmitted to the entire body; so automatically it increases the efficiency of the brain.

Also, we should know that the fourth layer of the brain cortex deals with connections and separations of the body, which is 60% of all problems.

Through the message given to the entire body, it helps the body to grow and become aware of the external problems which helps the body to heal beautifully.

Sound healing vibrations help a body to increase the efficiency of the brain cell as it renders a calming and soothing effect to our brain to get relaxed, especially through all kinds of water music and water frequency, which help our body to get relax and calm.

8.3 Decreases the Period of Treatment

Because sound healing therapy works in the sonic mode, it takes less time to treat than other therapies. Once the root problem or targeted area of physical pain, or the emotional blockage is deducted the process of treatment becomes very easy.

Not only this but we receive a lot of information, in the form of thoughts. Some information or thought which carries the vibration can be productive for us, while some information (vibration) in the form of thought is not comfortable to our cells resulting in some disease. Once we recognize the thoughts which are making our body uncomfortable, sound healing works on those particular areas and thoughts through the vibrational mode. The beauty of sound healing therapy is that whether the body wants to take this therapy or not, the sound will still produce the desired effect.

The time duration of this therapy completely depends on the person's problem and his/her surrender to the therapy.

8.4 Economical Therapy

Apart from the expert sessions, sound healing is something which can be used in your daily routine because the sound is something which you can hear daily in the form of thoughts.

So, the very first step is **to become aware of your thoughts**. Once you know which thoughts are disturbing you, you can filter them on the spot. Then half your problems are solved.

Sound healing synchronizes brain waves to achieve profound states of relaxation, helping to restore the normal vibratory frequencies of the cells in our bodies

SOUND OF INFINITY BAND
VIRTUE. VALUE. VICTORY

Secondly, start a daily practice of meditation like **chanting of OM mantra** or any other mantra that you feel a connection with. Such chanting will help your cells to get back into a rhythmic pattern. This you can do anytime, anywhere according to your lifestyle.

Thirdly, **listening to water music** or sounds related to water can help you a lot as they help to repair the inside water cells of your body.

These are some easy tips and techniques which help your body to get rid of toxic thoughts and vibrations that come from the external source and also in form of verbal thoughts or assumptions thought.

09

CONCLUSION

Sound healing therapy improves physical and emotional health and wellbeing. The vibrations coming through the sound healing bowl mainly affect the mind, body, and soul. The sound coming from 20 musical instruments give a great impact on brain waves to relax them and heal their traumas.

Listening to pleasing sounds or repetitive tones is associated with flowing stress, reducing blood pressure, and helps one enter a state of relaxation. Vibrations and music have been used to heal for centuries. We used sound and music for healing purposes since ancient times from birth to death. Sound and music are so much connected with the human that on every occasion whether it's happy or sad, we perform sound and music ceremonies.

A sound wave can also slow down the heart rate and respiratory rate by creating a therapeutic effect on the mind and body. When the brain wave and body are synchronized and balance is restored and stress is released. A frequency of 174 Hz reduces pain and gives your organ a sense of security, safety, and love.

Sound healing works from gross to a subtle level, from simple emotional thought to physical disorder. Also, it allows the body to heal itself by slowing down the brain waves which affect each cell of the body shifting it from **disease to ease.**

So it is correctly said that sound healing therapy will be the "**MEDICINE FOR FUTURE.**"

SNIPPETS FROM SOCIAL MEDIA

डॉ. अंजू शर्मा को इंटरनेशनल हेल्थकेयर अवार्ड्स में मिला हेल्थकेयर एक्सीलेंस अवार्ड

पूर्व भारतीय कप्तान सुनील गावस्कर ने किया सम्मानित

जयपुर। हाल ही मुंबई में आयोजित हुए इंटरनेशनल हेल्थकेयर अवार्ड्स में साउंड मास्टर डॉ. अंजू शर्मा को हेल्थकेयर एक्सीलेंस होलिस्टिक वेलनेस-साउंड हीलिंग ऑफ द इयर 2021-2022 के लिए सम्मानित किया गया है। पूर्व भारतीय कप्तान सुनील गावस्कर ने उन्हें सम्मानित किया। देशभर में साउंड हीलिंग के क्षेत्र में उत्कृष्ट कार्य करने के लिए उन्हें यह अवार्ड मिला।

गौरतलब है कि डॉ. अंजू शर्मा पिछले काफी समय से साउंड बाउल हीलिंग थेरेपी के द्वारा लोगों की शारीरिक व मानसिक समस्याओं के उपचार पर कार्य कर रही हैं। देशभर के कई बड़े संस्थानों में उनके द्वारा साउंड बाउल हीलिंग थेरेपी की वर्कशॉप आयोजित की गई हैं। उन्होंने आर्मी कैंपस से लेकर जेलों में कैदियों तक लिए साउंड हीलिंग सेशन किए और उन्हें साउंड की मदद से अपनी मानसिक व शारीरिक समस्याओं को ठीक करने को लेकर जागरूक किया। वहीं कोरोना की पहली व दूसरी लहर में उन्होंने सोशल मीडिया के माध्यम से ऑनलाइन लाइव सेशन कर कई लोगों को मानसिक परेशानियों से उबरने में भी मदद की। होलिस्टिक वेलनेस में यह सब कार्य करने के लिए उन्हें यह सम्मान दिया गया।

साउंड बाउल हीलिंग थेरेपी के बारे में उन्होंने बताया कि हमारे शरीर में 70 प्रतिशत पानी है और अगर अपने ऑर्गन का मूल भी खोजें तो वह भी पानी से ही बने है। ऐसे में हमारे शरीर में 90 प्रतिशत पानी माना जा सकता है। यह तकनीक वाइब्रेशन और फ्रीक्वेंसी पर काम करती है। हमारे शरीर के सेल्स में ये वाइब्रेशन पहुंचती हैं और उन समस्याओं को दूर करती हैं जिससे हम परेशान हैं। एक से डेढ़ घण्टे के कुछ सेशन में आप उस समस्या को जड़ से ठीक कर सकते हैं।

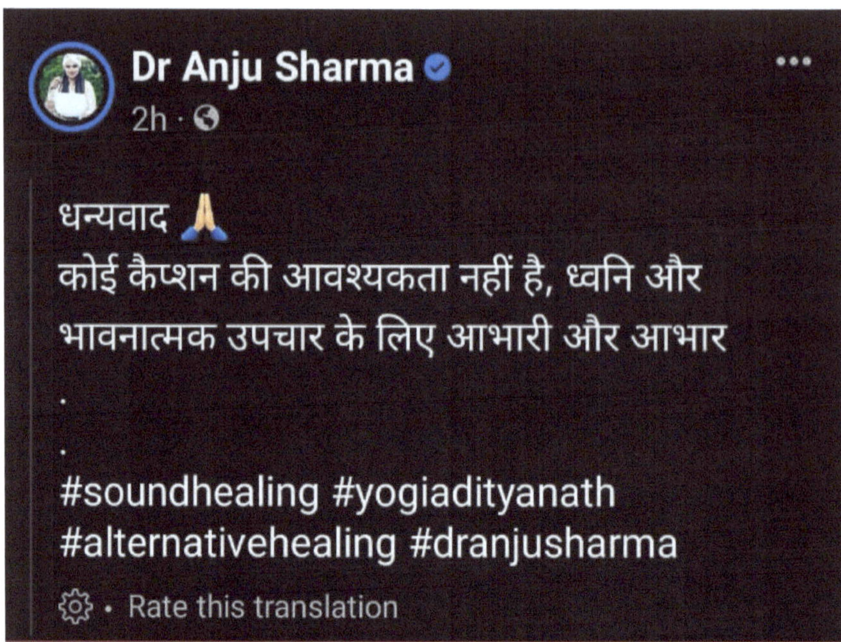
Dr Anju Sharma
2h ·
धन्यवाद 🙏
कोई कैप्शन की आवश्यकता नहीं है, ध्वनि और भावनात्मक उपचार के लिए आभारी और आभार
.
.
#soundhealing #yogiadityanath #alternativehealing #dranjusharma
Rate this translation

DAILY DIGITAL EDITION
ASIAN LITE
LONDON · DUBAI · DELHI · NEW YORK · SINGAPORE

www.asianlite.com TUESDAY, OCTOBER 13, 2020 ASIAN LITE P27

Following the success of their healing song, Asia's first musical healing band, 'Sound of Infinity' band, has come up with their second music single, which launched on October 10 during the Mental Health Week.

The video of the music single was shot in Dehradun, near a waterfall and a river, as the band has used natural water sounds. The music also features instruments like rainstick, bamboo rainstick, ocean drum, crystal bowl and a very high resonance of gong.

As per the makers, the music is focused on water frequency.

"The idea of creating this music is to enhance the water element in the human body, which has more than 70 percent water. Every day we take in thousands of thoughts which travel in our body. Our thoughts affect our body's cells. We get to know about these aftereffects when the cells get distorted in physical forms like cyst, tumour or clot or bigger diseases. If we are uncomfortable with a particular thought, then that is affecting our body. You cannot control your surroundings but whatever you are receiving your body is taking and you can control that by working on the water element," said the makers.

There are various types of water sounds like, waterfall, raindrops, water flowing from a tap. Even seawater has a different sound.

"So this particular sound heard in the music, helps to heal one's core issues, basic survival, and also the guilt factor and their absorption and suppression. This music piece is a combination of these frequencies or chakras. Just listening and watching this music can bring a difference. If one listens to this sound regularly, the cells which had been distorted can be repaired," said psychic reformer and sound and energy master Dr Anju Sharma, who founded the band to make people aware that they can cure and heal themselves through music and various frequencies and its vibrations.

This, claims Dr Sharma, is also helpful for people with infertility issues. "Women who listen to this music during ovulation can experience the effects in their body. This is because you are cleaning the water within. Taking a practical example, when you see clean water you feel good whereas when you see dirty water you want to stay away from it. And the work of water is to flow if it stops.

Therefore, with these frequencies we are making the water clean which will help you to think big, grow big and able to attract abundance in life. Your mind will be clean. The combination of frequencies will affect pancreas, intestine, stomach, uterus and most importantly kidneys. Furthermore, if a person is diabetic or has sugar craving will see the impact of this music. This music is also beneficial for men with low sperm count," she shared.

Celebrating Mental Health Week, Dr Sharma also organised a series called 'Let's Talk Dil Se' in which she had a heart-to-heart conversation with various people from different walks of life like homemakers, doctors, entrepreneurs and kids. Each session focused on the effects of the pandemic on their mental health and how one can deal with it and cure it.

डॉ अंजू शर्मा ने तिहाड़ के कैदियों को दिया साउंड हीलिंग सेशन

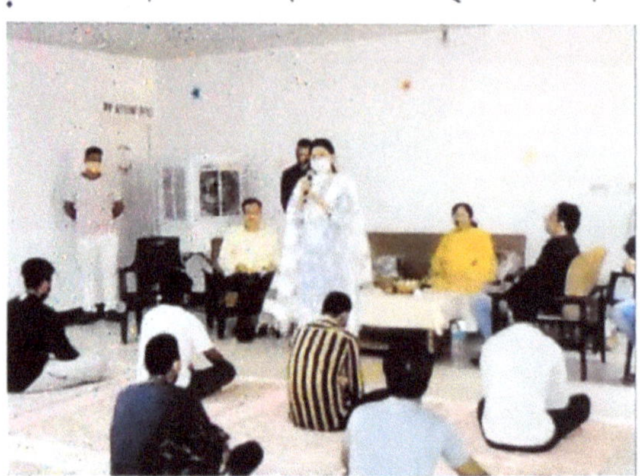

नई दिल्ली, (वीअ)।आज के समय में, ध्यान, दिमागीपन और विचारशील अभ्यास हर दिन उनके सामने आने वाले पागलपन और तनाव से लड़ने की कुंजी साबित हुए हैं। इस मुद्दे को संबोधित करते हुए, प्रसिद्ध मानसिक सुधारक, साउंड एंड एनर्जी मास्टर, वेलनेस-होलिस्टिक कोच, इंटरनेशनल स्पीकर और साउंड ऑफ इन्फिनिटी नामक म्यूजिकल हीलिंग बैंड की संस्थापक डॉ अंजू शर्मा ने 'ध्यान और मानसिक शांति की भूमिका' पर एक कार्यशाला आयोजित की। तिहाड़ जेल संख्या-४ में जेल बंदियों के लिए कार्यशाला का आयोजन उत्तर-पश्चिम जिला विधिक सेवा प्राधिकरण द्वारा किया गया था। एक घंटे तक चलने वाली इस कार्यशाला में लगभग 100 से अधिक कैदियों ने भाग लिया। सत्र की शुरुआत विचार प्रक्रिया पर चर्चा के साथ हुई और विचार प्रक्रिया किसी व्यक्ति के जीवन को कैसे बदल सकती है। इस चर्चा के दौरान, डॉ अंजू शर्मा ने पांच इंद्रियों और भावनात्मक स्वतंत्रता तकनीक पर कुछ प्रकाश डाला। उन्होंने चर्चा की कि कोई अपनी भावनाओं और विचार प्रक्रियाओं पर कैसे काम कर सकता है। उन्होंने अपनी आंतरिक दुनिया को जानने पर भी जोर दिया कि उनके शरीर और दिमाग में क्या चल रहा है।

संवादात्मक कार्यशाला के दौरान, कैदियों को यह समझा गया कि उनकी नकारात्मक विचार प्रक्रिया ने उन्हें जेल में डाल दिया है। उन्हें सलाह दी गई कि वे खुद से प्यार करना सीखें और नकारात्मक को एक सकारात्मक विचार प्रक्रिया में परिवर्तित किया जा सकता है जो उनके भविष्य को उज्ज्वल करेगा। बाद में, एक ध्वनि ध्यान का आयोजन किया गया जिसमें सभी ने ध्यान किया और अपने मन और शरीर पर ध्यान केंद्रित किया और मन को शांत करना सिखाया। कार्यशाला के दौरान व्यक्ति के अपराध-बोध को कम करने के लिए क्रिस्टल बाउल, रेनस्टिक और हिमालयन तिब्बती बाउल जैसे कुछ उपकरणों का उपयोग किया गया।

कार्यशाला का निर्देशन तिहाड़ जेल अधीक्षक पवन कुमार ने पहली बार सजायाफ्ता कैदियों के लिए किया था। इस कार्यशाला का उद्देश्य इन बंदियों को अपने अंदर की भावना से अवगत कराना और उन्हें यह समझाना था कि उनका जीवन उन्हीं के हाथों में है।

उपचार

ध्वनियों के सम्मिश्रण से रोग प्रतिरोधक क्षमता भी हो रही है मजबूत, कई डॉक्टर सोशल मीडिया पर कर रहे हैं लाइव सेशन

नाद योग के संग दिल्लीवाले लड़ रहे कोरोना वायरस से जंग

संजीव कुमार मिश्र • नई दिल्ली

कोरोना ने दिल्लीवालों की दिनचर्या बदल दी है। चौक चौराहों पर लगने वाला मजमा अब कम हो गया है। गली मोहल्लों में किस्से कहानियों की महफिल भी कम सज रही है। महामारी के दौर में जिंदगी घर की दहलीज के अंदर सिमट गई है। स्वास्थ्य से लेकर आर्थिक परेशानियां बढ़ी हैं, नतीजा हताशा और चिंता भी बढ़ी है। लेकिन नाद योग इस मुश्किल घड़ी में बहुत मददगार साबित हो रहा है। कई डॉक्टर भी सोशल मीडिया पर नाद योग संबंधी लाइव सेशन कर रहे हैं, जिसका लोग भरपूर फायदा भी उठा रहे हैं। ध्वनियों के सम्मिश्रण से हताशा और निराशा से न केवल पार पाया जा रहा है बल्कि रोग प्रतिरोधक क्षमता भी मजबूत हो रही है।

ध्वनि तरंगों से प्रभाव: साउंड एंड एनर्जी विशेषज्ञ डॉ. अंजू शर्मा बताती हैं कि नाद, ध्वनि होती है और योग अपने शरीर के अंदर झांकने की प्रक्रिया है। तनाव आदि, ध्वनि के जरिये ही हमारे शरीर के अंदर प्रवेश करता है। ध्वनियों का तालमेल गड़बड़ाने पर ही शरीर पर प्रभाव पड़ता है। विचार ध्वनि रूप में शरीर के अंदर प्रवेश करते हैं। ये ध्वनियां या बातें कोशिकाओं पर असर डालती हैं। मान लीजिए, आपसे किसी ने कहा कि आप के समक्ष ये विकट समस्या है या आप किसी अमुक चीज में कमजोर हैं। यह बात तब तक आपको प्रभावित नहीं करती, जब तक कि आप इसे मानसिक रूप से स्वीकार नहीं करते हैं। एक बार आप मान लेते हैं कि आप में कोई कमी है तो कोशिकाएं भी तनाव में आ जाती हैं। यह मानसिक विकार के रूप में सामने आता है। लॉकडाउन में चिंते, आर्थिक, बीमारी से लेकर तमाम चीजें हैं जो मानसिक विकार का कारण बन रही हैं। इस भावनात्मक और मानसिक रूप असर पड़ता है।

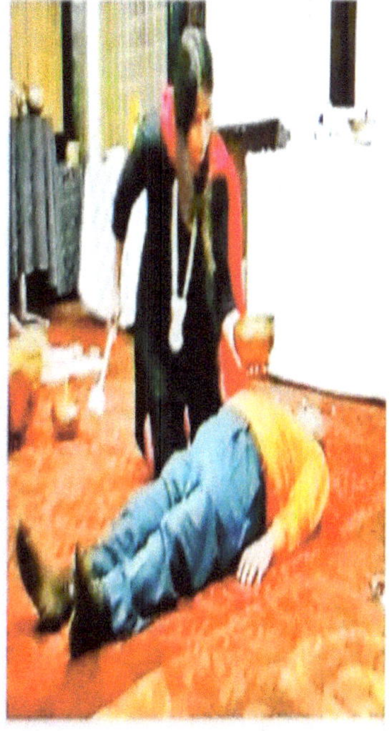

नाद योग के दौरान तिब्बतीयन हीलिंग बॉल्स से ध्वनि उत्पन्न करतीं डॉ. अंजू शर्मा • सौ स्वयं

कोरोना काल में हताशा, निराशा और अवसाद को दूर करने में मददगार साबित हो रहा है नाद योग

ध्वनि यज्ञ भी कारगर

मुताबिक अंजू, जनता कर्फ्यू तो याद ही होगा। जब प्रधानमंत्री नरेंद्र मोदी ने कोरोना वॉरियर्स के सम्मान के लिए ताली, थाली आदि बजाने पर जोर दिया था। दरअसल, योग की भाषा में वो ध्वनि यज्ञ था। यह हम घर में इस तरह के यज्ञ को बार बार करने की सलाह देते हैं। इसके जरिए ध्वनि उत्पन्न की जाती है। जिससे तनाव समेत बैक्टीरिया आदि चमत्कारिक रूप से खत्म होते हैं। यह एक घंटे का होता है।

कैसे असर करता है

मुताबिक डॉ. अंजू शर्मा हम मंत्र, ध्वनि, फ्रीक्वेंसी, वाइब्रेशन आदि के जरिये कोशिकाओं को दुरुस्त करते हैं। इसके लिए हम हिमालयन क्रिस्टल बॉल्स, तिब्बती हीलिंग बॉल्स, योग आदि का प्रयोग करते हैं। हम इससे दो तरह की ध्वनियां निकालते हैं। ओंकार (20 से लेकर 20 किलो हर्ट्ज तक की ध्वनि) और इन्फ्रासोनिक। मंत्रों के उच्चारण पर हम अधिक जोर देते हैं। इससे मानसिक शांति मिलती है। मुताबिक डॉ. अंजू फेसबुक, यूट्यूब पर हम नाद योग संबंधी लाइव सेशन भी करते हैं। जिसे काफी लोग पसंद भी कर रहे हैं।

www.jagran.com

ध्वनि के आवेग से मनोविकार का उपचार

राष्ट्रीय ज्योतिष सम्मेलन

साउंड बाउल हीलिंग थैरेपी का प्रदर्शन

डेली न्यूज, जयपुर। शास्त्री नगर स्थित क्षेत्रीय विज्ञान पार्क में आयोजित राष्ट्रीय ज्योतिष सम्मेलन में शुक्रवार को ज्योतिषीय गणनाओं और ग्रह नक्षत्रों की दशा की विवेचनाओं के बीच उस समय माहौल कुछ अलग नजर आया, जब एक व्यक्ति को एस्ट्रोलॉजी की एक नई तकनीक से सांसारिक दुनिया से अलग कर दिया गया। एस्ट्रोलॉजर ने साउंड बाउल हीलिंग थैरेपी का प्रदर्शन कर वहां मौजूद लोगों को अचंभित कर दिया।

सम्मेलन के दूसरे दिन दिल्ली से आई डॉ. अंजू शर्मा ने इस नई ज्योतिषीय विधा का प्रदर्शन किया। इस दौरान उन्होंने ज्योतिषियों में से

दुनिया से अलग हो चुका है।

दांपत्य को लेकर विशेष विवेचनाएं

डॉ. अंजू ने बताया कि यह पद्धति शरीर व मन के विकारों को दूर करने के काम आती है। सम्मेलन के बीच यह तकनीक आकर्षण का केन्द्र रही। अखिल भारतीय प्राच्य ज्योतिष शोध संस्थान की ओर से आयोजित सम्मेलन में ज्योषियों ने दाम्पत्य जीवन व उससे जुड़े पहलुओं की ज्योतिषीय विवेचनाएं

क्या है साउंड बाउल हीलिंग

डॉ. अंजू शर्मा ने बताया कि यह तकनीक वाइब्रेशन और फ्रीक्वेंसी पर काम करती है। हमारे शरीर की कोशिकाओं में इन तरंगों का कंपन पहुंचता है और उन समस्याओं को दूर करता है, जिससे हम परेशान हैं या मन व शरीर में कोई विकार आ रहा है। तीस से चालीस मिनट में इस विधा के जरिए अलग-अलग सेशन में आप उस समस्या को जड़ से ठीक कर सकते हैं।

A LEADING BUSINESS NEWS PORTAL

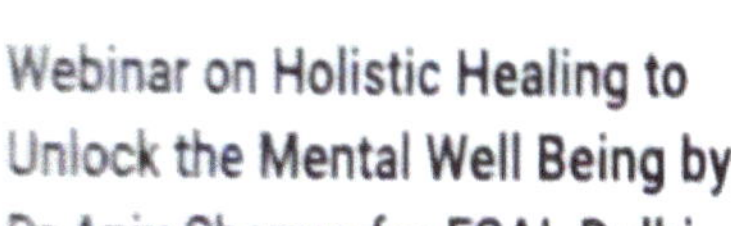

Webinar on Holistic Healing to Unlock the Mental Well Being by Dr Anju Sharma for FSAI, Delhi Chapter

> Health > Webinar on Holistic Healing to Unlock the Mental Well Being by Dr Anju Sharma for FSAI, Delhi Chapter

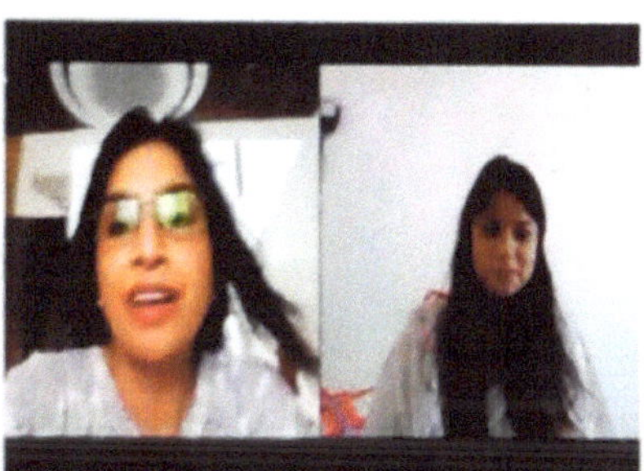

New Delhi: With pandemic and daily increasing cases, are impacting everyone's mental well-being. The uncertainty prevailing related to the health, money or job creates an

Dr Anju Sharma who is also an international speaker highlighted on how due to the outbreak of COVID-19, almost all the people are in a stressful environment which is creating psychological chaos. Each person reacts differently to a given stressful situation. Dr Anju Sharma shared tips to deal with such situations and how to improve the immunity system. During the webinar, she also discussed the water

aspect of your body and how it helps in improving your mental and physical well-being. Dr Anju also did some practical session of breathing techniques before concluding the webinar. The breathing exercise helps to enhance the quality of life. Everyone breathe but do we focus on our breathing. It helps in

managing your mind and will also help you relax both mentally and physically.

This webinar was free for member of FSAI / CTBUH / IIA / IIID / ISHRAE / ASHRAE / GACS / APA ASSOCHAM GEM / IGBC / IFE-UK / IEEMA / ASIS / OSAC.

DR ANJU SHARMA | FSAI DELHI CHAPTER | HOLISTIC HEALING | MENTAL WELL BEING

PREVIOUS
7 Stress Management Techniques Every Teacher Should Know

NEXT
Experience IPL with TCL's latest QLED TV Available at Exciting Prices

FEATURED RESOURCES

newindianexpress.com

'Your brain is better on music': All the benefits it has

By Nikita Sharma | Express News Service | Published: 04th March 2020 08:08 AM

Anju Sharma with two of the musical instruments she uses in her healing practice.

महोदय,

आपको विदित कराते हुए अपार हर्ष हो रहा है कि इस वर्ष आगामी 11 अगस्त को पहली ब
उत्तराखंड से प्रसारित होने वाला इकलौता न्यूज चैनल HNN 24x7 "उत्तराखंड एजुकेशन एक्सीलेंस अ
का आयोजन करने जा रहा है। इस सम्मान से उत्तराखंड में शिक्षा के क्षेत्र में अभूतपूर्व कार्य करने व
हस्तियों को नवाजा जाएगा। जिसे भारत सरकार के मानव संसाधन मंत्री श्री रमेश पोखरियाल निशंक
और माननीय मुख्यमंत्री उत्तराखंड श्री त्रिवेंद्र सिंह रावत अपने कर कमलों से देंगे।

महोदय, हम आपके द्वारा साउंड एंड हेल्थ के क्षेत्र में अभूतपूर्व व उत्कृष्ट योगदान देने के
आपको अवॉर्ड से सम्मानित करना चाहते हैं। आपसे निवेदन है कि उक्त समारोह में पधारने हेतु हम
निमंत्रण स्वीकार कर आप हमें कृतार्थ कीजिएगा।

REFERENCE

- Patanjali Yog Sutra
- Literature of sound
- Article by Deepak Chopra
- Yoga Nidra
- The seven spiritual laws of the universe
- Sound medicine
- Sound of Infinity Band Workshops
- Article published in newspapers
- Music sound capsule
- Quantum physics
- Katha Upanishad
- Shvetashvatra Upanishad
- Bhagavad Gita
- German medical science

ABOUT THE AUTHOR

Dr Anju Sharma is an award-winning doctor, psychic reformer, sound and energy master, motivational health awareness Speaker, wellness-holistic coach, and founder of the musical healing band Sound of Infinity. She holds a Doctorate in Sound Healing. Her decade-long journey in alternative medicine and healing therapies engage with the nuances of different dimensions of wellness.

Registering the effect of something as subtle as water frequencies on the human mind, her work takes healing into the realm of sensoriality, spirituality and the subconscious. Dr Sharma's healing touch has helped 3000 plus clients gain back equilibrium and take their mental and physical health on a higher plane.

Having been an international speaker at many workshops with students of schools and universities, prisoners and corporate professionals to her credit, Sharma is also a certified trainer in neuro-linguistic programs, with over 10 years of experience in the field of healing, health and holistic wellness.

She specializes in 128 traditional and international healing modalities and therapies such as sound, colour, hydro, art, verbal, non-verbal, and emotional freedom technique (EFT), among others.

As a wellness researcher, her study of the subconscious mind and thinking ability adds weight to her credibility as a multi-hyphenate healer. She is also a certified aromatherapist, master trainer in scientific vastu healing, as well as a master in hypnosis.

Anju Sharma has been honoured in 2018 by the Uttarakhand CM for her Incredible Work in field of Alternative Medicine & Healing and her anti-drug campaign. In 2022, she received Pioneer Award for Divine Science (Sound & Mantra Healing) Excellence by CM of UP Shri Yogi Adityanath.

The awards won by her include HealthCare Excellence Award 2021-2022 awarded by Sunil Gavaskar, Inspirational Woman Of The Year, 2022 by MTTV Media for creating awareness about mental and emotional health, Sound Queen Award by International Astrological Conference in Dubai. She has been awarded at the National Well-being Summit 2021.

In 2021, she received acknowledgement from Tihar Jail for training prisoners on emotional health and way of processing healthy lifestyle. She was honoured by District & Sessions Court Judges for delivering a powerful talk on Women's Day 2020.

She was also nominated for the "Marvellous Book Record" of the world. She has also been felicitated and awarded for her research work on Sub-consciousness, Mind, Thinking Ability, Perception and Consciousness. Her main approach is to create abundance with health.

www.ingramcontent.com/pod-product-compliance
Lightning Source LLC
LaVergne TN
LVHW021252160826
845679LV00001B/46

9798887049007